D1783690

Table of Contents

Unsolved 1943

- Baby
- Maurice Stuart Horner
- Marguerite Huber
- Florence Mary Needham and Nicholas John Benjafield
- Mary Elizabeth Comins
- Baby
- Maureen Ritchie
- John Neill
- William Olding
- John Henry Hillman
- Joseph Powell
- Gladys Merrick
- Thomas Hayes
- Charles Gallagher
- William Pearce
- Jan Von Der Spek
- Baby
- Baby
- Frederick James Pollington
- James Patrick OConnor
- Baby
- Stephen Emerton
- Annie Lewis

Unsolved 1943

A list of unsolved cases for 1943.

Madge Knight

Age: 43

Sex: female

Date: 6 Dec 1943

Place: Manor Cottage, Aldingbourne

Madge Knight died from burns that were thought to have been caused by corrosive acid.

An open verdict was returned at her inquest.

She was the wife of a retired architect and surveyor who she married in September 1934. They were said to have been perfectly happy together.

They shared their house with Madge Knight's sister and her husband who had a room together. Madge Knight and her husband had a room but Madge Knight sometimes slept in a small occasional room.

The husband said that He had sat with Madge Knight alone on the night of 18

November 1943 from about 7.45pm until 10pm when he went to bed. He said that he was told the following morning that Madge Knight's back was all burnt. He said that they couldn't make out what had happened. He said that after he was told, he could find no burnt or scorched clothing in the house and added that as far as he was aware, no acids were kept in the house.

When the husband was questioned, he said that they didn't quarrel at all, but said that Madge Knight had been very strung up and said that he simply sat in a chair and listened to her. He said that she 'held forth' for about an hour and that she was overwrought. He said that when he went to bed at 10pm he left Madge Knight in the lounge and didn't see or hear anyone else that night.

It was noted at the inquest that the husband was said to have told a policeman he thought that he had heard Madge Knight's sister and husband return at about 10.30pm, but when questioned at the inquest he said that he didn't remember hearing them.

The husband noted that Madge Knight drank heavily, saying that she would have five or six whiskies in the course of the evening and then a nightcap with her sister and her husband, however, he said that he could not say that she was not sober on the night of 18 November 1943, but did say that he thought that she was rather excited. He said that he thought it was the work that Madge Knight did that was responsible for her outbursts, adding that she did the sweeping and dusting as they could not get a maid, and said that her health was not what it was.

Madge Knight's sisters husband said that he and his wife were awakened by Madge Knight screaming between 3.30am and 4am, saying that she was in her bed, covered by her bedclothes, but not wearing her pyjama jacket, and said that the skin on her back was peeled. He said that they called a doctor later in the morning between 7am and 8am.

The sister's husband said that Madge Knight and her husband had been to London that day and that when they had returned Madge Knight had been very upset because her husband had told her that he would put her brother up as a director on his Water Board but that someone else was elected.

Madge Knight's sister and her husband both said that they would not say that Madge Knight was sober nor that she was drunk.

Madge Knight's sisters husband denied at the inquest that he had done away with any of Madge Knight's clothing or bedding and denied that he had been in Madge Knight's bedroom that night.

A doctor said that when he received the first message to call round to see Madge Knight, that it didn't seem urgent and didn't go around until he got a second message at about 11am which stated that Madge Knight was in great pain. He said that when he saw Madge Knight and asked her how the burns had happened, she replied several times that she had nothing to tell him.

When Madge Knight's burns were examined by a dermatologist from Harley Street in London, he said that they were burns of some nature, but that he could only hazard what the cause was, although said that he thought that some corrosive liquid might have been poured over her back.

Madge Knight was admitted to St Richards Hospital in Chichester on 2 December 1943 and died four days later on 6 December 1943 from toxaemia following extensive burns.

A pathologist at the Royal Sussex County Hospital in Brighton that examined her injuries said that if corrosive fluid was used, that it might have been self-inflicted if she had been sitting and had fallen back into the bath, noting that two bruises on her shoulders could have been caused in that way.

A police detective sergeant said that he found no stains on the floors of the house and no trace of any burning or staining of clothing or furnishings, nor anything that had contained acid.

When the coroner summed up he said that some features of the case were not entirely satisfactory, noting that the statement of Madge Knight's sister's husband at the inquest conflicted with the one that he had previously made to the police and signed, and said that that did not impress. The coroner also noted that if Madge Knight had been heard screaming between 3.30am and 4am, being obviously in great pain, then why was the doctor not called for another four and a half hours, and even then, without any urgency.

The coroner then returned an open verdict, stating that that was due to the conflicting nature of the evidence.

George Edward Hulme

Age: 25

Sex: male

Date: 6 Dec 1943

Place: Centenary Hall, Poole, Dorset

George Edward Hulme died from a fractured skull he received mysteriously in a lavatory at a dance hall.

He was a soldier and had been out drinking with a friend.

A corporal said that he went out with George Hulme on 3 December 1943 to several public houses where they had drinks and that after that they went to the Centenary Hall where a dance was taking place. He said that after they arrived and bought tickets they went into the lavatory, however, he said that whilst in the lavatory, he turned around and saw George Hulme lying on the floor. He said that he then carried him downstairs and took him home by train.

At the inquest the coroner asked the corporal, 'Did it occur to you that he might have been attacked by someone?', to which the corporal replied, 'No'.

The corporal noted that George Hulme might have hit his head on a ledge when he fell in the lavatory.

The manager of the Centenary Hall said that he saw the corporal helping George Hulme down the stairs at the dance hall, saying that the corporal told him that he was taking George Hulme out for some air, and that when they got outside he saw the corporal slide George Hulme down, and that as he did so, he heard a terrific crack, and added that there was no doubt in his mind that that was caused by George Hulme hitting his head on the blast wall. However, a man in the Royal Navy said that he had helped to get George Hulme down the stairs at the dance fall and said that he was quite sure that George Hulme had not banged his head against the blast wall when they got out.

The corporal said that he carried George Hulme back to the station and took him on the train back to his house and said that whilst doing so he had no recollection of George Hulme banging his head on the way. He said that he had no recollection of George Hulme banging his head against the blast wall when he was put down, or falling off his shoulder and banging his head. He said that he had tried to revived George Hulme when he found him on the floor in the lavatory, but without success. He said that as he carried him to the station on his shoulder, George Hulme slipped off once, but said that only his feet touched the ground. He said that when the train arrived, he had assistance in getting George Hulme out of the train and that he telephoned for transport to get him home and that when they got back George Hulme's brother helped to undress him and put him to bed.

The corporal said that it wasn't until later that he heard that George Hulme had died.

George Hulme's brother said that the corporal woke him up bringing George Hulme home and told him that George Hulme had passed out through drink and that they then put George Hulme to bed. However, he said that when he was later awakened by George Hulme's irregular breathing, he called for a doctor.

The manager of the Centenary Hall said that after he saw George Hulme carried out by his friend, he asked the doorman how he had come to let George Hulme into the dance in the condition that he was in, and said that the doorman replied, 'It's the quickest one I have ever seen. They were all right when they went in'.

A gunner said that he helped the corporal to put George Hulme, who was unconscious, onto the corporal's shoulders and said that he then followed them for a while. The gunner said that at one-point George Hulme fell off the corporals shoulders and that there was a thud as though he had fallen on his head.

A doctor that examined George Hulme said that he found no bruise or external injury visible on George Hulme's head and said that he thought that some injury must have been caused in the lavatory. He said that some degree of violence would have been needed to have caused George Hulme's skull fracture, but that it was difficult for him to associate it with his head hitting the blast wall. He said that he could not see how George Hulme could have hit his head on the rough brick blast wall with sufficient violence to cause his injury without leaving any external marks.

George Hulme died from cerebral abrasion and hemorrhage due to a fractured skull.

An open verdict was returned.

Rose Ada Robinson

Age: 63

Sex: female

Date: 28 Nov 1943

Place: John Barleycorn Beerhouse, 518 Commercial Road, Portsmouth

Rose Ada Robinson was found strangled in her pub, the John Barleycorn Beerhouse in Portsmouth on the 29 November 1943.

A 47-year-old man was tried twice for her murder but acquitted. At his first trial at the Winchester Assizes on 14 March 1944 the jury failed to agree. At his second trial at the Old Bailey in London on 4 April 1944 he was acquitted.

The John Barleycorn Beerhouse at 518 Commercial Road in Portsmouth had been entered between 11pm on 28 and 8.30am on 29 November 1943 through a window at the rear which was broken. The window had been broken and then the window catch was released and the window then opened and climbed though.

Rose Robinson was later found strangled on the floor of her bedroom. Her handbag and the drawers in her bedroom had been ransacked and it was believed that a substantial sum of money, around £400 in £5 and £1 bank notes, silver and copper, had been stolen.

A detective sergeant that went to the John Barleycorn Beerhouse at about 10.20am on 29 November 1943 said that he found Rose Robinson in the back bedroom on the first floor lying on her back with the bottom of her head resting against an angle of the wall about two or three inches from the floor. She was clothed in a blue and white spotted dress, the bottom of which was drawn up round her body to within approximately four inches of her private parts. Beneath her body there was a rug, a portion of which lay in a fold beneath her back. He said that a stocking and a pair of stays lay on the floor near her right shoulder and that a pair of bloomers were lying on the floor about two feet away by a chair that was facing away from her body and about two and a half feet from it.

The detective sergeant said that the bedroom was in a state of confusion and that the dressing table had been moved out from the wall at one end for a distance of about one foot and that the top-dressing table drawer was slightly open. He also added that the contents of both of the top-dressing table drawers appeared to have been ransacked.

He noted that there was a rug on the floor between the bed and the dressing table and another smaller rug by the side of the bedroom door, both of which appeared to have been disturbed, when they were found.

He said that the bed clothing was in considerable disorder and amongst the bedding and nearby he found several handbags and other items on it. They were:

- Exhibit 9: handbag that was open but had no money in it but contained a quantity of papers.
- Exhibit 10: handbag with no money in it.
- Exhibit 11: an empty purse.
- Exhibit 12: handbag.
- Exhibit 13: leather shopping bag that contained six threepenny pieces, an elastic band, three farthings and two unlit candles with keys attached to it.

- £1 and a 10/- treasury note folded up together with some coppers.
- Exhibit 14: six blue money bags and a green money bag were also found amongst the bedding and on the floor.
- Exhibit 15: twelve elastic bands were also found amongst the bedding.
- Exhibit 16: lying on the outer covering of the bed and mixed up with the other clothing was an eiderdown.
- Exhibit 17: a piece of cloth fabric was found lying in the bed amongst the folds of a knitted coverlet towards the end of the bed.
- Exhibit 18: a blackout blind was found lying on the floor near the foot of the bed. The blind had apparently been wrenched from its roller that was still in position over the window.
- Exhibit 19: the blackout roller from above the window.

When the police later questioned Rose Robinson's son, he said that Rose Robinson slept in the back bedroom at the pub on her own and stated that he knew that Rose Robinson kept her money in two handbags, exhibits 9 and 13 and that she paid the brewers each month in cash. He said that he used to do her books for her and said that her gross takings were about £50 per week and that at the time of her death that she would have had about £400 in notes in the house which he said she kept in a bundle with an elastic band round them.

When the police made a further examination of the premises, they found a window behind the bar of the bar parlour in which one pane had been broken near the catch. When the police examined the sill on the outside below the broken pane they found a black button with some thread attached to it.

The police also noted that there was a window in the bottle and jug department that faced the private bar and the entrance to the yard which was also broken. It was a sliding window that was also a sort of hatchway.

A doctor said that he formed the opinion that Rose Robinson had probably stumbled, possibly on her knees, to get to a window and that in doing so she had struck her brow and face. He said that he then thought that she rolled onto her back and that whilst on the floor her assailant had either sat on or kneeled on her and strangled her with his right hand.

The man that was tried for her murder was arrested on 21 December 1943 after he was questioned by police who suspected him of selling stolen property in a refreshment house. When he was questioned about some shoes, he was selling he confessed to Rose Robinson's murder.

When the man that confessed to Rose Robinson's murder was first seen at St Mary's Prison in Portsmouth at 3pm on 22 December 1944 his clothes were taken for examination. When he took off his jacket, he said, 'It's all right, Inspector, you won't find any buttons there. After I did the job I found I had a button missing so I got the wind up and when I got back to London I pulled them all off'.

The police later found a piece of knotted thread in a fold of the lining of the man's left sleeve opposite the division at the cuff which was taken away for examination along with the button and other items.

The man's right hand was also photographed to be used as evidence as he had all his fingers missing, and moulds where made of it from which plaster casts which were then made and sent of for examination.

The man that was tried made three confessions on three occasions after handing himself in on 21 December 1943 in London but later said that they were bogus and denied murdering Rose Robinson in court. It was also seen that he had all his fingers missing from his right hand.

The confession that he made on 22 December 1943 read:

'I cannot remember the name of the public house. I think it was named the Fox. It was in Commercial Road. I cannot be sure of the date I broke into the public house, but I think it was on 28th November. When I climbed over the wall at the back of the public house I had a look round the gardens. I got into a house and as I could not find the bar I came out again into the garden. I then went to a window at the back of another house and got in through a window into a bar. I went upstairs and looked in several rooms. In the back room I saw a woman. There was no light in the room, and I flashed my torch on to her. She must have heard me and got out of bed as she was wearing some clothes. She asked me who I was. I did not answer her and she started to scream. I went for her and grabbed her by the throat with my right hand. She fell down near a window and as she fell the blackout fell down from the window. I held her down on the floor and then I covered her face over with a piece of cloth I found in the room. There were two large handbags on a dressing table with a glass top. These bags were full of money. When she screamed, she rushed towards the bags and tried to grab them. I tipped the money out of the bags into my overcoat. There were a lot of silver and five-pound notes and one-pound notes. I noticed that the old lady was not wearing any rings. I did not take any jewellery. I unbolted the back door and went into the yard, then into an empty house next door. Through this house and into the street I jumped into a motor car which was waiting for me and went away. I do not want to say anything about the car or who was driving it. I left Portsmouth and went straight back to London. I did not count the money, but I think I had about £450 in notes and about £20 in silver. About £300 of this sum was in £5 notes. When I got back to London, I gave £50 to a young lady and the rest of the money I kept in a suitcase. I remember when I left the public house there was a woman came out of a house near the pub. I heard accidently that the old lady had died in Portsmouth and since this time I have not been able to sleep and have been drinking heavily. I cannot remember everything very clearly, but I did not mean to kill the old lady and I am very sorry. I told the young lady who I was with that if ever I was arrested, she was to take the suitcase and money and go away. She saw me arrested in London on 21st December and I gave her the tip to go. I do not wish to give any information about the young lady or the man who drove the car'.

When the police from Portsmouth went to London on 21 December and saw the man that had confessed he was cautioned and when cautioned he said, 'That is all true, don't you think I did it?' and the police replied, 'I can't tell you what I think, but some enquiries will have to be made before I take you back, Perhaps you would care to tell me what happened'. The man then said, "Yes, when I got upstairs in the public house I saw a woman in the back room and as she screamed I grabbed her by the throat and she fell down near a window and as she fell the blackout fell down. I held her on the floor, and I thought she had fainted. She looked awful so I covered her face with a piece of cloth I took off the bed'. The man then asked, 'Did the old lady have a bad heart?' and the police told him that they could not say. The man then said, 'I can't understand it as she went quiet straight away. I know I took a lot of money out of some bags on a dressing table and got out of the pub'. The man was then asked if he would like to make a statement which he said he would.

After the man made his first statement, he was asked whether he wanted to read it but said that he didn't and so it was read out to him. When he went to sign it he asked that both the policemen present sign it and when he was told that it didn't matter whether the other sergeant signed it, the man was said to say, 'I want to put your names in as the law is a funny thing and two are better than one'.

After he signed his first statement he said, 'What a funny thing. A woman with all that money not having a ring on her finger'.

After he appeared before the Justices on 5 January 1944 the man asked to see the Chief Constable and said to him, 'I want to help you all I can Chief and if you can arrange for me to be taken to London I will go to a house where there is a suitcase with some of the money in it and also to a cafe where I will point out the other man who came to Portsmouth with me when I did the job'. However, he didn't give any indication as to the whereabouts of the suitcase or the cafe and when questioned on that he said, 'It may mean bringing the woman in and I don't want you to do that'.

On 7 January 1944 the police took the man to a cafe in Waterloo Road, but after some time there the man said, 'It doesn't look as if the man is going to turn up. Let us go in the public house next door'. The name of the public house next to the cafe was the Hero of Waterloo. After about half an hour in the Hero of Waterloo, the man didn't indicate that the man that they were looking for was there, after which the man took the police to a house in Clapham Common where he said he would recover the suitcase, however, he neither found the suitcase nor any money at the house and he was then brought back to Winchester.

When the police spoke to people that knew Rose Robinson, they spoke to a man that lived on Knox Road in Stamshaw, Portsmouth who had known Rose Robinson for about 36 years and who had been helping her at the John Barleycorn for the last three and a half years. He said that he helped her on the evening of Sunday 28 November 1943, having got there at about 7pm and said that the house closed at 10pm. He said that the two front doors were bolted and that the back door was left until about 10.15pm. He said that the back door was at the bottom of the stairs and that he bolted it at about 10.15pm.

He said that the hatchway of the bottle and jug department was used and that people got into that department from the yard from Grafton Street. He said that the door leading from the yard to the bottle and jug department was shut but not locked, and also said that the hatchway was shut and locked by jamming a mallet into the side. He added that the window of the bar parlour at the back was locked and that he saw that it was locked. He added that there was a door that led from the passageway to the yard in Grafton Street and that he padlocked that door from the outside and then left the premises between 10.30pm and 10.35pm by the public bar door into Commercial Road, saying that Rose Robinson let him out. He said that she then shut the door after him and that he then heard her put the catch up and the bolt.

The man also confirmed that Rose Robinson kept her takings in the handbag, Exhibit 13, saying that she would roll the notes and put elastic bands round them and added that she would put the silver into bags similar to Exhibit 14 and then into the bag Exhibit 13.

The man added that he could not say how much money Rose Robinson would have had on the night of 28-29 November. He also added that he had never seen her wearing jewellery and that he had seen her with two rings a long time before.

A woman who lived in Washington Road in Portsmouth and who was employed as a charwoman at the pub said that she went there everyday to work. She said that at the time of her death that Rose Robinson slept in the back bedroom and confirmed that she kept her money in two handbags, Exhibits 9 and 13, which she said she kept under her eiderdown at the foot of her bed. She said that she cleaned her back bedroom out at various times and said that there was a piece of looking glass on the top of the dressing table and that the table was flat against the wall. She also added that the blackout was one roller blind. She also said that she had never seen Rose Robinson wearing any rings.

The woman said that she arrived at the John Barleycorn Beerhouse at 8am on 29 November 1944 and knocked at the door and rattled the letter box but got no reply. She noted that that had happened on several occasions previously and that she then walked up and down outside for nearly an hour before she saw the man that lived next door who then let her in. She said that they went in together and found Rose Robinson dead and then called the police.

Rose Robinson was actually found by the next door neighbour who had let the charwoman in . He said that he lived at 520 Commercial Road in Portsmouth and was a stoker in the Royal Navy. He said that at about 9am the charwoman came to his house and that as a result of what she said he got over his back garden wall and into the yard of the John Barleycorn and found that the back door was halfway open. He said that he then went into the the John barleycorn and then opened the front door and let the charwoman in and then went upstairs and stood at the doorway to the back bedroom and looked in and saw Rose Robinson lying on the floor. He sid that he didn't see her face, but then went back downstairs and called the police.

A man that was employed as a Fire Watcher by Messrs Brickwoods at their bottling store in Grafton Street said that on the night of 28-29 November 1943, he had been on duty, starting at 6pm. He said that between 3.30am and 3.45am, he heard some unusual sounds whilst he was in the bottling store coming through Grafton Street from the direction of Elm Road towards Grafton

Avenue. He said that they were either the sound of a person walking with either heavy boots or walking heavily and that as they passed the store, he heard someone muttering to themselves. He said that as the person got by the gateway, he heard them messing about with the palings outside the store which was next door to the back entrance of the John Barleycorn. He said that he then went out with his torch and shone it through the palings and that after that he didn't hear anything more from that direction.

However, he said that a little while after that, about a couple of minutes, he heard the smashing of glass which came from behind him as he stood looking into Grafton Street, which he said would have been from the back entrance of the John Barleycorn, but that after that he heard nothing more.

A woman who was living at 514 Commercial Road on the night of 28 November 1943 said that she had been sleeping in the front bedroom at the time when between 1am and 3am she was wakened by a banging on the kitchen window at the back which knocked the blackout down. She said that she then heard some heavy footsteps in the kitchen and listened for a little while but heard no more. She said then, that at about 2.30am she heard more footsteps going round the outside of the house and through the passage at the side and round the front. She said then that at just before 3am she got out of the front window and saw a motor car and four men between her house and the John Barleycorn Beerhouse. She said that she then got back into her bedroom.

The woman said that when she went into her kitchen the next morning, she found the blackout, which was a piece of three plywood over the window, had been broken and was laid outside. She added that the table had also been moved a small distance away from the wall and that the back door was half open, noting that she had bolted it the night before when she went to bed and said that it was clear that someone had unbolted it during the night. However, she said that she didn't miss anything.

It wasn't until 21 December 1943 that the man who confessed was arrested. He had been at a refreshment house at 106 Waterloo Road in London at about 4.30pm trying to sell people a pair of shoes when a plain clothes policemen who had been keeping watch on him with another policeman for an entirely different matter approached him. After they approached the man and took him to a police box in Waterloo Road they said that when they told the man that he was taking him to the police station the man said, 'I am wanted for things far more serious than this. The Yard wants me. It is the trap door for me now'. After asking the men if they were policemen and the policemen showed him their warrant cards, the man said, 'I am glad you picked me up, it will do you good'. He was then taken to Kennington Road police station and on the way, he handed one of the policemen a silver box and said, 'This is a Christmas Box for you. I know this will be my last Christmas'. When he was searched at Kennington Road police station he said, 'The shoes and silver box came from the job at Woking and cigarette case came from the job at St Albans'. He later said, I am glad I am in. I have been through hell for the past three weeks. I have been a bastard all my life and I will finish as I lived. I was sorry for it the moment I had done it. I haven't slept since. It preyed on my mind. She must have had a weak heart. Poor old girl'.

The doctor that examined the body of Rose Robinson said that in his opinion she had died from asphyxia due to manual strangulation. He said that he thought that she died some time early in the morning of 29 November 1943 during the course of an assault on her and not sometime after the assault. The doctor also examined plaster casts of the right hand of the man that confessed to Rose Robinson's murder, which had all its fingers missing and said that in his opinion that the strangulation marks that he found on Rose Robinson's neck could clearly have been caused by the man's hand. He said that although it was deformed, its dimensions were adequate, stating that the stumps of the index, middle and little fingers were sufficiently long and capable of the stretch necessary to effect the grip around Rose Robinson's neck.

At the second trial at the Old Bailey the man said that he didn't do it and said that he could not have done it as he had not been there and had spent the night of the murder in an air raid shelter in London. The police said that the man had said things in his confession that only the murderer would have known, but the man said that the confessions had been prepared by the police for their own ends.

The court heard that the man admitted to leading a life of crime and having told many lies since he was arrested for the murder. However, the jury was told that if they thought that because of the man's hand deformity that he would have been unable to strangle Rose Robinson that that would be the end of the case. The jury spent 65 minutes deliberating and returned with a not guilty verdict.

Norah Irene Bartlett

Age: 33

Sex: female

Date: 18 Nov 1943

Place: Rhydings Park Road, Singleton, Swansea

Norah Irene Bartlett was found dead in a lane near her home in Rhydings Park Road, Swansea on the Thursday night of 18 November 1943.

The police stated that Norah Bartlett's death was due to foul play.

She had been sexually assaulted and strangled. There were no external marks of violence on her body other than a few scratches on her face.

It was thought that she was last seen in the company of an American soldier.

The police said that they were anxious to trace the identity of a girl and an American soldier who had been out walking in Rhyddings Park Road at about 10.45pm on the Thursday night and who had been approached by a young lady. It was said that as a result of what the young lady had told them that they both then looked into a front garden on the west side of the street where the American soldier shone a torch on a person lying there.

The police also said that they were interested in tracing a workman who had been carrying firewood and who had entered Rhyddings Park Road from King Edward Road at about 10.50pm on the Thursday. It was said that the workman had been stopped by the same young lady who had asked him to shine his torch on a person that had been lying in a front garden of one of the houses at the lower end of Rhyddings Park Road, third or fourth from the end, on the west side.

Following her murder and an increase in the number of attacks on people in dark streets, Swansea Council was urged at a meeting to apply to the Minister of Home Security for permission to introduce modified street lighting.

Norah Bartlett was later buried in Mumbles Cemetery.

She worked as a canteen worker in Swansea and had lived with her widowed mother at Rhydings Park Road.

Rita Irene Stephens

Age: 21

Sex: female

Date: 17 Nov 1943

Place: Lydney

Rita Irene Stephens died from a septic abortion.

She had lived at 27 Queen Street in Lydney.

Her death was said to have been due to peritonitis caused by a septic abortion.

She had gone to Gloucester on 17 October 1943 saying that she was going to see friends and was away for about four or five days. She then returned home one night but said that she was going away again and went off again for a further few days. Her grandmother, with whom she lived in Queen Street said that when she returned after that she looked very unwell and said that Rita Stephens told her that she had a cold.

Her grandmother said that on Tuesday 10 November 1943 she treated Rita Stephens for her cold and said that she did not appear to get any worse, but said that the following day, 11 November 1943 she didn't seem so well and when she appeared worse in the evening she called for a doctor.

After Rita Stephens's grandmother called for the doctor, Rita Stephens told her that she thought that she might have had a miscarriage, saying that she had fallen and had had a good shaking and that three or four days later the miscarriage had occurred.

The doctor said that when he was called to see Rita Stephens on 12 November 1943 during morning surgery, he found her very seriously ill and ordered her removal to hospital where she had local and general treatment to reduce severe toxaemia.

The doctor said that on the Monday, 16 November 1943 her condition was growing worse and that he thought that an operation was imperative, and it was carried out the same afternoon. He said that following the operation she held her ground fairly well and was quite comfortable when he saw her at 11pm but said that he was summoned a few hours later at 1.30am on the Tuesday 17 November 1943 when her condition took a turn for the worse. He said that he then ordered treatment for her and sent for her relatives and that she rallied for a time, but then suddenly died at 2.45am.

When the coroner summed up at the inquest, he said that there was no evidence to show how her death was brought about.

Mary Elizabeth Giblin

Age: 47

Sex: female

Date: 6 Nov 1943

Place: Beverley Road, Hull

Mary Elizabeth Giblin was knocked over by a car on the Beverley Road near Hull.

Following her death, the police released the following notice:

'At about 10.15pm on Saturday, November 6, 1943, a woman, Mary Elizabeth Giblin, residing at No. 32, May Street, Hull, was knocked down while crossing the Beverley Road, Hull, near to Beverley Road Baths, and received injuries which had since proved fatal. The vehicle concerned is a small dark-coloured four-seater saloon motor car, and was travelling out of the city towards Beverley. The driver did not stop and the car is likely to be damaged at the front. Will the driver of the car, or any person who witnessed the accident, please communicate with the Chief Constable, City Police, Hull, telephone Hull Central 16000, or any police constable'.

She had been talking to her husband and some friends at the time she was hit on the Saturday night 6 November 1943.

She died from an extensive fracture of the skull and laceration of the brain and other severe multiple injuries. The doctor that examined her body said that he didn't think that she had been run over by the car.

Mary Giblin's husband, who was a chipper and painter employed by Messrs Joseph Rank Ltd, said that they had gone to the Rose Hotel public house on Beverley Road and had stayed there until about 10pm. He said that they were quite sober when they left and that they stood outside talking with some friends for a while and that as they were moving away he saw a motor car flash past and felt Mary Giblin knocked violently from his side. He said that at the time he heard a loud bump and saw Mary Giblin flung towards Grove Street. He added that she landed about 10 yards from where he had been standing.

He said that the saw the car travelling fast towards Newland, closely followed by another car that he believed was blue in colour. He said that by the light of the second car he saw that the first car was yellow and said that it was a fairly larged sized saloon car. He added that he was unable to see the identification marks.

Mary Giblin's husband said that he accompanied Mary Giblin to the infirmary where she was pronounced dead.

At the inquest, Mary Giblin's husband said that visibility had been good at that night, about 60 yards, and said that no warning was given by either of the cars.

The day after Mary Giblin was knocked over, a woman who lived in Greenwood Avenue in Hull said that she and her sister and a friend had engaged a taxi at Paragon Station and had passed the Rose Hotel on the Saturday night. She said that the car was a small old-fashioned type of car and that she sat in the front seat. she said that as they passed the Rose Hotel she felt a bump as if something had hit the car, and that the car then began to make a funny noise. She said that she asked the driver to stop but said that he did not do so. She added that at the same time that she felt the bump she saw something whiz by.

The woman said that when they left the car in Greenwood Avenue, she noticed a delve in the near side mudguard. She said that she then saw the rear identification plate with the registration number 8434 which she then wrote down on a piece of wallpaper whilst her sister paid the fare of 4s 3d, including a tip of 6d. However, she said that she did not think that should would be able to identify the driver again.

Another one of the women that had been a passenger in the taxi gave similar evidence and when she was asked at the coroner's inquest what conclusion she came to after discussing the matter with the other passengers later, she said that she was sure that they had hit something. She then said that the following morning when they went to work they heard some other girls talking about the accident and decided that as soon as six o'clock came that they were going to report it, stating that they had made their minds up that the car that they had been in had been the car that had hit Mary Giblin. She said that when she heard that the incident had happened outside the Rose

Hotel, that they knew that it must have been the car that they had been in.

A policeman said that when he went to inspect motor car WF8434, he found that it was damaged, saying that there was a dent in the mudguard and a number of fabric marks, including yellowish-green wool fibres identical with the surface fibres of the green coat that Mary Giblin had been wearing at the time she was knocked over.

The owner of the car who lived in Mayfield Street, was a long distance motor driver, however, when the police questioned him he said, 'I have never had this car out since I purchased it', adding that he kept it a garage in Albany Street and that it had been there on the Saturday night, 6 November 1943, along with his employer's motor lorry.

He said that the damage to the car had been caused on the Saturday morning when he had knocked into it with his lorry as he was starting it up.

However, the coroner said that he considered that it had been proved beyond doubt that his car was the one that had knocked Mary Giblin down.

When the car owner was questioned, he agreed that the car was in running order on the Saturday 6 November 1943, but that he had never driven it mechanically on the road at any time.

The inquest also heard that the car and the lorry were both kept in the garage but that it was not big enough for both vehicles and that one of them, depending on which one had gone in first, would be left protruding through the garage doors meaning that the garage could not be locked securely.

However, it was also heard that his mother and his wife both confirmed that the car owner had been with them on the Saturday night at the Eagle Hotel in Spring Bank until closing time. The car owner said that after they left he accompanied his wife and mother to their home and then went off to his own home and was in bed at 11pm.

When the coroner summed up he said that he had no choice but to return an open verdict, noting that the car owner had an alibi.

He said that there was the possibility that due to the fact that the car had been left in the garage without the door being locked that someone might have taken it out, but he said that he thought that if it had been taken out by an unauthorised person that he would hardly expect them to have taken the trouble to return it and risk being caught, noting that the ordinary tactics of car thieves was to abandon cars after exhausting the petrol. He also noted that on the night of Saturday 6 November 1943 that the car had been used as a taxi and that the only return that the driver had got from it was apparently 3s 9d and a tip of 6d. As such, he said that it took a lot to believe that the car had been taken out by an unauthorised person but that as far as the evidence went that he had no alternative but to return the open verdict.

William Ritchie Chalmers

Age: 31

Sex: male

Date: 7 Oct 1943

Place: Grimsby

William Ritchie Chalmers died from phosphorus poisoning.

He was a gunner.

He had gone to the cookhouse to make some cocoa for the night watch. He then became ill and was put to bed.

A sergeant said that they had all drunk the cocoa that William Chalmers had made for them without suffering any ill effects.

The following morning an ambulance was called to take him to the hospital, but he died before arriving.

Following his post-mortem his death was stated to have been due to an irritant poison but although tests had failed to establish the nature of the poison, it was thought that there was every indication that it was phosphorous.

His Captain said that a phosphorous preparation spread out on papers in the officers' mess had been used to kill beetles. He said that the paper slips were gathered up each morning and destroyed. He added that William Chalmers had no access to the phosphorous.

William Chalmers was described as a non-smoker, a non-drinker, a good athlete and a good soldier.

He was from Kirkcaldy and had been a joiner before joining the army 15 months earlier.

He was good at football and whilst in Barrow-in-Furness he had been on Barrow FC's book and later played for Bournemouth and Raith Rovers.

Caroline Ellen Traylor

Age: 18

Sex: female

Date: 22 Sep 1943

Place: 94 Foord Road, Folkestone

Caroline Ellen Traylor was murdered between 13 and 17 June 1943.

Her dead body was found during a police search strangled in a bombed-out shop passage on Foord Road in Folkestone a short distance from her home in Sussex Road on 17 June 1943 at about 11.30am.

The pathologist said that she had been strangled by a grip of considerable force.

Caroline Traylor's body was found by a policeman during a search of unoccupied buildings by the police looking for her. A policeman said that he entered 94 Foord Road by a gate entrance off Devon Road. He said that the back door was closed, but not locked and that when he went in, he saw a blue suede shoe lying on the floor and then to the left of the entrance a large brown leather handbag. He said that he then saw Caroline Traylor lying on the floor in a passage from the shop doorway.

A 24-year-old soldier in the Royal Artillery was convicted of her murder in September 1943 at the Old Bailey and sentenced to death but his conviction was quashed on appeal on 1 November 1943.

At the time of the murder the soldier had been at a camp about five miles from Folkestone and had been in the Mechanic's Arms public house with a friend and had got back to camp late.

The grounds of his appeal were misdirection of the jury by the judge. It was heard that the judge had commented in his summing up on the fact that when the soldier was arrested, he had not denied the charge but had instead said that he would take advice. It was said that what the judge had said was tantamount to saying, 'If a man says, 'I reserve my defence', then you may rely on that as evidence showing that he is the man responsible for the crime charged'.

Caroline Traylor was a cinema usherette and she had been on duty at the cinema on 13 June 1943 until about 9pm and it was thought that she had gone straight to the Mechanic's Arms public house after leaving work. It was said that the soldier had met Caroline Traylor in the pub and had got into conversation with her. The soldier had been with another soldier at the time, but after the soldier was said to have started speaking to Caroline Traylor, he felt that he was in the way and said that he then left their company. The other soldier said that he went back to camp in a truck at about 10.15pm.

Two trucks had brought the two soldiers, as well as others into Folkestone on the evening of 13 June 1943 and the second truck later left Folkestone on the return journey at 11.10pm with all soldiers other than the soldier tried for Caroline Traylor's murder accounted for.

However, at the trial it was heard that there was no one to say that Caroline Traylor and the soldier had been together after they left the public house at 10pm.

However, several witnesses that had known Caroline Traylor said that they had seen her walking about with a soldier after she left the pub. She was seen by one witness at about 10.15pm walking along Bradstone Avenue towards Black Bull Road with a soldier which was near to the bombed out shop where she was later found.

Caroline Traylor was also later seen at 10.30pm with a soldier in St John's Church Road and then again at 10.40pm talking to a soldier outside the shop where she was later found murdered.

The soldier himself later returned to camp at about 1.30am on 14 June 1943. He said that he had walked back to camp, having met an officer in the WAAF who he had walked back with as far as the bus station. The police later spoke to an officer in the WAAF who said that after she had arrived at Folkestone Junction station at 12.15am, a soldier had followed her and caught up with her.

Evidence against the soldier included a rust or orange coloured wool fibre that was found on one of Caroline Traylor's torn fingernails which corresponded with fibre in a khaki shirt that had been worn by the soldier. However, at the trial the soldiers defence said, 'You might find an orange thread of similar fabric on some 5,000,000 shirts today'. The defence also added that there was nothing on the soldier's clothes to connect him with being in the shop where the murder took place.

Police also found six dark hairs on her body and it was noted that she herself had auburn, sandy-coloured hair. The six dark hairs were later said to be identical in every way with the hair of the soldier.

The police said that they also found a sandy coloured hair on the soldier's uniform that they said corresponded in every respect with the hairs taken from Caroline Traylor's body.

The soldier was detained in London by the US Army Police on 30 June 1943. He was a married man who had two children and whose home was in Santley Street in Longsight, Manchester.

After the soldier was arrested it was heard that he had made various inconsistent statements regarding what he had done on the evening of 13 June 1943.

It was also stated that the soldiers behaviour following the murder up until the time he was arrested was also suspicious as it was alleged that he had endeavoured to hide his identity as much as possible because he must have known that he was wanted for interview.

It was also noted that a book of leave forms was also taken from the soldier's troop office and it was later found in his possession. It was heard that two of the documents were filled up and bore the signature of an officer which was not the officer's signature that the name related to. It was also found that other articles, including the soldier's pay books were also missing and that four pay books belonging to other soldiers were also found on the soldier, one of which had belonged to one of the soldiers roommates. It was also noted that the soldier had gone so far as to extract his photograph and to have put it in another man's paybook.

It was also heard that on 18 June 1943 that the soldier had told another soldier that he was going home for the weekend as he suspected his wife's conduct, although it was noted at the trial that in his wife's interest, there seemed to be no foundation for that suggestion.

On the same day, 18 June 1943, the soldier was found by his sergeant major to be away from his vehicle. It was found that after being paid he should have attended for guard duty at 7pm but that he was nowhere to be found and that the reason for that was because he had taken the 8.40pm train from Euston to Manchester.

On 19 June 1943 the soldier was with his wife in Manchester and was wearing civilian clothes. It was later heard that the soldier had gone to see his mother-in-law with his wife and that they both appeared to be worried and that he told them that he was on embarkation leave. The mother-in-law said that as her daughter was looking poorly she remarked that perhaps she was worried that her husband was going abroad and said that the soldier said, 'Not so worried as me'. However, it was also noted that there appeared to be no suggestion of any trouble between him and his wife. It was heard that when they later went out for drinks the soldier said that he had had a bit of bad luck over the previous three weeks, but that he didn't say what that was.

On 20 June 1943 the soldier was in Stockport where he saw a friend who he told that he was due back in Folkestone at midnight. However, it was found that he spent the night of 20-21 June at a drill hall at Mere.

On 22 June 1943 the soldier was at Stafford railway station where he met a woman and told her that he was a fighter pilot in the RAF and they later went to Birmingham together where they spent the evening at a cinema.

The next day, 23 June 1943, the soldier went to London with the woman who lent him an attache case because he told her that his luggage, which was supposed to have arrived at the station, had not.

The following day, 24 June 1943, the soldier telephoned the woman and made an appointment to return the attache case, but he failed to show up.

The soldier was next heard of at the Queen's Hotel in Leicester Square, London on 28 June 1943 in the company of a Canadian soldier. Whilst there he got into a conversation with two US NCO's and spent the night with them at the Green Park Hotel.

He was arrested the following day, 29 June 1943 at the City of Quebec public house and taken to Marylebone Police station where he was held until police officers from Folkestone could arrive. A policeman said that he had been on duty at Marble Arch when a man attached to the CID of the US Army communicated with him and he went off with him to the City of Quebec public house where he saw the soldier. He said that he asked the soldier what his name was and said that the soldier gave him a false name. He said that he then grabbed the soldier by the left arm and told him that he answered the description of a man that was wanted for the larceny of a wallet and contents as well as questioning by the Folkestone Police and said that the soldier replied, 'You have got nothing on me'.

When the police arrived, he admitted that he had been with Caroline Traylor, but then said, 'I want to be fair with you and to myself but before I make a statement I should like to get advice'.

The police then took possession of his army uniform in Manchester. They later also went to the Imperial Hotel in Russel Square where they found several AB64 forms in various names which were leave forms.

When the soldier was questioned, he admitted being with Caroline Traylor, but said that after he had come out of the pub with her he had kissed her but that she had told him that she had a date to keep and so he left her. He said that he then walked home and on the way met the WAAF officer whose bag he offered to carry.

The doctor said that the cause of Caroline Traylor's death was manual strangulation. He said that her throat injuries consisted of bruising and tearing of the skin as by the fingernails at the level of the voice box on both sides, left and right. He added that there was a fracture of the voice box on the left side and bruising between the voice box and the spine. He said that her injuries to the back of her neck consisted of a single bruise as from a thumb high up under the head and immediately to the left of the mid line and that there were three similar bruises as from the strong pressure of avering fingers further round the right side of her neck.

He added that there were bruises to her brow and to her chin that were in keeping with her head having been forced back and downwards onto some surface during the grip.

The soldier's trial at the Old Bailey had lasted three days.

Caroline Traylor was married but lived at home with her parents in Sussex Road, Folkestone. Her husband was a sergeant in the Durham Light Infantry and had been serving in North Africa at the time.

Donald Yates Grant

Age: 25

Sex: male

Date: 22 Sep 1943

Place: Guards Depot, Caterham, Surrey

Donald Yates Grant died from a fractured skull after he was hit over the head with a rifle butt by another soldier.

The other soldier said that he had been cleaning his rifle when he had raised it to throw it over to the next bed when he hit Donald Grant in the head with the butt. He said that there had been no quarrel and that he had had no intention of hitting Donald Grant with it or throwing it at him.

An open verdict was returned when the foreman of the jury stated that there was insufficient evidence to show exactly what happened.

Donald Grant was from Sale in Cheshire.

Baby

Age: 0

Sex: female

Date: 27 Aug 1943

Place: Victoria Main Line Station, London

The body of a newly-born female child was found in the ladies cloakroom by a cleaner at Victoria Main Line Station behind some pipes in a cubicle.

It was wrapped up in brown paper.

The police said that there were no marks of violence on the body and nothing on the wrappings to assist them in tracing the child's mother.

When the cloakroom attendant was asked whether he had noticed anyone in particular carrying a brown paper parcel into the cloakroom, he said that probably a hundred or more people came to the cloakroom during the day carrying a parcel or suitcase.

The pathologist said that the child weighed 5lbs 10oz and that there was no natural condition to account for its death which he said he thought was due to inattention at birth.

Mabel Harper

Age: 53

Sex: female

Date: 13 Aug 1943

Place: Western Avenue, Cardiff

Mabel Gwendoline Harper was found gagged and stripped on the grass verge of Western Avenue in Cardiff on the morning of 13 August 1943.

She was found with her clothing torn to shreds and with her ankles tied together with her stockings.

She also had severe facial injuries.

She had lived in Aubrey Avenue, Victoria Park in Cardiff.

She had been out visiting friends about a mile away from where she was found on 12 August 1943 and it was thought that she was attacked whilst walking home after having missed the last bus.

It was said that the route that she would have walked home would have been pitch black in the black-out and that the main road that she had walked along was bordered by high trees.

Her brown fibre attache case and black handbag were missing.

The police said that soldiers on late pass on the night were being questioned.

It was thought that a man had witnessed her murder and the police called for a man that was seen standing on the kerb in Western Avenue opposite the grass verge where Mabel Harper was murdered at about the same time to come forward.

Mabel Harper had three children, two of whom were in the forces. She was a widow.

Skeletal Remains

Age: 0

Sex: male

Date: 26 Jul 1943

Place: Plough Hotel, Cheltenham

The skeletal remains of a newly-born child were found during demolition work at the Plough Hotel in Cheltenham.

It was wrapped up in newspaper that was dated 1915.

The remains were found by a bricklayer on 26 July 1943 as he was engaged in repair work at the pub which had recently been damaged by fire. He had been demolishing a lath and plaster wall between 2.45pm and 3pm in a small passage between what had previously been rooms 15 and 16.

He said, 'I noticed a small parcel resting between the wall and a small cupboard adjoining. This had obviously been used by housemaids, for there was a quantity of ashes and small coal above and below the parcel, and there was a dustpan and several pieces of cloth there. I pulled the parcel out and found that it contained a small skeleton. I thought it was the carcase of a foul'.

A policeman that examined the parcel said that the bones were wrapped in brown paper and within the wrappings he found a quantity of small pieces of newspaper that appeared to have been torn and nibbled by mice. He said that with some difficulty he was able to piece together portions of the newspaper and found that it was a copy of the Daily Telegraph dated Wednesday, June 15, 1915.

The policeman said that there was a label on the brown paper that was addressed to a notable character in the district who had been a frequent visitor to the hotel and who was addressed on the label by a former title. He added that there was also another label on the bearing the name of Liptons, Ltd and addressed to a woman who was apparently a previous visitor to the Plough Hotel. When a local manager of Liptons, Ltd was shown the label he stated that that type of label had not been used for 25 or 30 years.

A pathologist at Cheltenham General Hospital said that the skeleton was that of a newly born full term child, but that he was unable to determine its sex. He added that there were no obvious signs of disease or of a cause of death.

The coroner recorded an open verdict at the inquest stating that there was insufficient evidence to show the identity of the child, its cause or time of death, or its sex.

Violet Farrell

Age: 29

Sex: female

Date: 9 Jul 1943

Place: 11 Bramwell Street, Sunderland

Violet Farrell died from an abortion, but there was no evidence to state whether it had been self-inflicted or caused by another.

The jury returned an open verdict after deliberations lasting two minutes.

Ellen Rosa May Sharp

Age: 32

Sex: female

Date: 8 Jul 1943

Place: 4 Linden Passage, Linden Gardens, Chiswick

Ellen Rosa May Sharp died following an illegal operation on 8 July 1943.

She was taken to the West Middlesex Hospital where she died, her death being due to toxaemia and haemorrhage following a septic abortion brought about by an instrument used by some person or persons unknown.

It was also stated at her inquest that the circumstances surrounding her death were not fully disclosed by the evidence and an open verdict was returned.

At the first hearing of her inquest on 16 July 1943, it was heard that there were signs that Ellen Sharp had definitely been interfered with and that any interference with a woman to produce abortion was a criminal offence and that if a person was killed as a result of that criminal action then it was a matter of murder.

Ellen Sharp lived with her mother in Chiswick.

Florence Paul

Age: 28

Sex: female

Date: 8 Jul 1943

Place: 121 St Olafs Road, Fulham

Florence Paul died from an abortion.

She died in Fulham Hospital on 8 July 1943.

Her husband was a private in the army and had been serving since 1941. He said that they had two children already and that he knew that she was in a certain condition.

The pathologist that carried out the post-mortem said that there was no natural disease to account for her death and that she had recently been pregnant but that the pregnancy had been terminated completely by an abortion. However, he added that there was no evidence of interference of any kind and nothing to distinguish it from a natural abortion.

He said that the abortion had been followed by an infection that had spread into her bloodstream which had then resulted in gas gangrene.

At her inquest, the coroner asked the pathologist whether the organism, or infection, might have been instructed by an instrument before the abortion and the pathologist replied, 'Yes'.

The pathologist agreed that her abortion might or might not have been natural.

Child

Age: 0

Sex: male

Date: 1 Jul 1943

Place: Stolford, Somerset

The body of a child was found in a cesspit in Stolford.

The body was found by a man on 1 July 1943 at Green Shutters in Stolford in a cesspit. The man said that he had been employed in emptying the cesspit when he saw some carpet and that when he took it out he saw the head and shoulders of a child in it.

At the inquest, a woman said that she had been the mother of the child, but the coroner intimated that he would not ask her anything.

A professor that carried out the autopsy said that he was not able to say whether the child

had been born alive as there were no organs
left.

The coroner returned an open verdict,
stating that there was insufficient evidence
to show if the child had been born alive.

Baby

Age: 0

Sex: male

Date: 16 Jun 1943

Place: St Laurence Church, Evesham

The body of a newly-born child was found in the porch of St Laurence Church in Evesham.

It was wrapped up in brown paper and left on a seat in the porch.

It was found by the caretaker on 16 June 1943 as he was working in the church grounds. He said that he entered the church at about 2pm to put his bicycle in the porch, at which time he said that he didn't notice anything being on the porch seats. He said that he then worked in the church grounds, during which time the church was unlocked, and that at about 5pm he went back in the church and noticed the brown paper parcel on the seat. However, he said that he thought that it had been left by mistake and left it there and locked the church up and went home.

However, he said that when he returned the following day he saw that the parcel was still there and so he thought that he had better take it to the police but before he did so he said that he undid the bottom end of the parcel and saw two feet of a child inside and so he put it back and reported it to the police.

The police arrived at the church at 8.45am on 17 June 1943 and inspected the parcel and untied it to reveal the body of a newly-born male child which they then took to the mortuary.

The body was wrapped up in a clean pillow slip and then wrapped up in brown paper.

When the body was later examined it was found to have no marks of violence on it.

Baby

Age: 0

Sex: female

Date: 10 Jun 1943

Place: West Country RAF Camp

The body of a newly born child was found in an air-raid shelter at a West Country RAF camp.

The body was found by an aircraftman who was cleaning out the shelter.

The post-mortem revealed that the child had breathed for a considerable amount of time. The doctor that examined the child said that it was a full-term female and that there were no marks of violence or injury on its body.

He said that whilst he could not state the definitive cause of death, it might well have been intention at birth.

At the conclusion of the inquest the coroner said that there was insufficient evidence to show the cause of death or her age.

Mary Josephine Rock

Age: 28

Sex: female

Date: 4 Jun 1943

Place: Townshend Court, St Johns Wood, London

Mary Josephine Rock died from an illegal operation.

She was a dancer and was found dead in a flat in St. John's Wood. She had lived in Edinburgh.

It was thought that she had come to London for the purpose of having the illegal operation. Her mother lived in London but said that Mary Rock had lived in Edinburgh since the start of the war, noting that she had come to London around Christmas time 1942 for a holiday, returning to Edinburgh in January 1943. Her mother said that Mary Rock had been an artist's model when the war broke out and had been employed at the Edinburgh College of Arts up until the time of her death.

A hairdresser who lived in Ullet Road, Sefton Park in Liverpool said that on 22 April 1943 she had come to London with an officer of the Royal Netherlands Navy and that they had stayed at the flat at Townshead Court. She said that two days after they arrived they saw Mary Rock in a bed sitting room of the flat and noticed that she looked very ill. She said that she arrived back at the flat with the naval officer just after midnight on Monday 26 April 1943, and that the following morning between 9am and 9.30am she heard the telephone ringing in the hall and said that when she went to answer it she saw Mary Rock lying in the hall.

After finding Mary Rock in the hall the naval officer then went off and got an RAF medical officer who was on duty at his station in St. John's Wood at about 11.40am on 26 April 1943. The medical officer said that the Dutch naval officer asked him if he would see a young woman in a flat nearby as she was either dying or dead, and said that when he got to Townshend Court he found Mary Rock lying dead on the floor of the entrance hall, and determined that she had been dead for about four hours.

A part-time canteen worker who had occupied the flat at Townshend Court since June 1942 said that two gentlemen rented rooms at the flat and that she first met Mary Rock when she came to the flat with one of the men that rented a room there in October 1942. She said that she met Mary Rock again around Christmas 1942 and then again on 10 April 1943 when she agreed to let Mary Rock have a room.

The canteen worker said that when she came home on 21 April 1943 at about 7pm she let herself in with her key and when she went in she saw the doctor coming out of her bed-sitting room, noting that she had never seen him before and that she was rather surprised to see him. She said that he said, 'Good evening' to her and then walked off out through the front door. The canteen worker said that she then went into the kitchen and put a kettle on the stove and then a few minutes later went into her bed-sitting room and saw Mary Rock seated on a divan there in her ordinary day clothes.

She said that she later went away on holiday at Easter, leaving on 23 April 1943, noting that it was the day after the hairdresser arrived to whom she had let have a spare room. She said that her holiday had been arranged some time before and that she had agreed with Mary Rock that she should look after her own room and get her own meals whilst she was away. She said that she worked between 2pm and 6pm daily and that the last time that she was in her room before going away was at about noon on Good Friday. She said that when she left there were no articles at the side of her bed. She said that a pail and basin were normally kept in the kitchen cupboard and her kettle was kept by the side of the gas stove. She said that when she left Mary Rock was in bed and seemed quite normal.

A GPO Clerk said that on 22 April 1943, £20 was paid into a Post Office Savings Bank book that had been issued at the Notting Hill Gate Post Office in the name of the doctor, but said that she could not remember who paid it in, or say how the £20 was made up.

The other man that had rented a room at the flat said that he had been there for about 11months, but that he had first met Mary Rock eight years earlier. He said that he met the doctor before the war but that the doctor had never attended to him personally, although said that he had once paid him a friendly visit at Townshend Court. The man said that at about 6pm on 21 April 1943 he had been in the hall of the flat making a telephone call when he saw the doctor letting himself out of the flat. He said that he was surprised to see the doctor, noting that he knew that the doctor was a friend of Mary Rock but that he wasn't expecting to see him there at that time. He said that it did cross his mind that the doctor might have been visiting Mary Rock in a professional capacity, noting that he knew that Mary Rock had been suffering with her chest.

The man said that later, just before 7pm, he saw Mary Rock in her dressing gown in the kitchen washing up some 'crocks' and noted that he thought that she looked ill. He said that he didn't know that she was pregnant.

At the inquest it was heard that the man's key had been found in the doctors possession and when asked about it he said that he had never sent or given it to the doctor and said that when he had gone away on 23 April 1943 he had left his key on the hallstand, noting that he returned on 26 April 1943.

It was determined that Mary Rock had died from acute general peritonitis due to septic instrumental abortion and that her injuries were caused by someone other than herself. It was noted that upon examination, it was found that her injury was found to have been caused with a degree of skill. It was stated that her injuries were consistent with an operation having been carried out upon Mary Rock on 21 April 1943.

A woman that had been living in Stanley Crescent in Notting Hill whose husband was serving in the Canadian Air Force said that she first met Mary Rock in June 1942 when she came to see her with a woman. She said that later, towards the end of March 1943, the woman and her mother, who was the doctor's daughter, came to see her again enquiring about a flat for Mary Rock. When the woman was asked at the inquest whether she knew why Mary Rock had come to London, she said 'Yes', and said that it was for an illegal operation. She said that she was asked to accommodate Mary Rock for a few days for that purpose but said that she refused to accede to the request, saying, 'I am not going to be drawn into anything connected with abortion', or words to that effect. She said that the doctor then told her that if anything did go wrong that there would be no evidence of interference.

However, the woman said that it was later agreed that Mary Rock could come to her flat for about a week, but just as an ordinary boarder and that it was understood that the doctor would not visit her. As such, she said that Mary Rock came to her flat on 2 April 1943 but said that she left again on 6 April 1943.

The doctor's daughter who lived in Lansdown Road in Holland Park, said that her father was a qualified medical man but that he had not practised since he had come back from India. As such, she said that he had no surgery or consulting room. At the inquest, she denied that she had made enquiries with the woman at Stanley Crescent for Mary Rock to stay for the purpose of an illegal operation and said that if her father, the doctor, had made any statement regarding no interference being found if something went wrong, it was not in her hearing. She added that she didn't know where the doctor had gone on 21 April 1943.

After the police found the body of Mary Rock at her flat, they kept watch in plain clothes and later arrested the doctor who they saw arrive at the flat with his attache case and let himself in with a key.

When he was searched, his attache case was found to have contained a steel knitting needle along with a stethoscope and thermometer. However, when he was asked by the coroner at Mary Rock's inquest whether he knitted, he said that he didn't, but that he used it to clean his pipe which he said was full of nicotine. He said that when he called at the flat he had been on his rounds, which included two chronic patients, and that that was why he had his case with him.

When the doctor was asked to give the names of the two other chronic patients at the inquest he said that he could not as they were patients with gonorrhoea. When the coroner asked the doctor whether he needed a stethoscope to treat men with gonorrhoea, the doctor said that he always carried a stethoscope.

A verdict of murder against a person unknown was returned.

Mary Rock was also known as Adele Russell.

Hannah Hudson

Age: 37

Sex: female

Date: 31 May 1943

Place: Willow Vale, Shepherds Bush

Hannah Hudson died from an instrumental abortion.

She died in Hammersmith Hospital a few days after admission from blood poisoning following a septic instrumental abortion.

Hannah Hudson's husband was a machine driller. He said that they had two children, one of whom was by Hannah Hudson's previous husband, and said that he didn't know that Hannah Hudson was pregnant.

He said that when he arrived home from work on 27 May 1943, he found her ill in bed and a doctor that was called out to see her had her removed to hospital.

A doctor at Hammersmith Hospital said that when Hannah Hudson was admitted she was admitted with a history of having a feverish chill and aches in her joints. He said that a provisional diagnosis put her illness down to acute rheumatism and said that an abortion was not suspected. However, he said that she had a sudden collapse and died on 31 May 1943.

The doctor that carried out Hannah Hudson's post-mortem stated that Hannah Hudson's illness was due to a septic instrumental abortion and that the interference must have occurred before 27 May 1943. He said that there was an infection that had spread to the blood stream and that her death was due to blood poisoning following septic instrumental abortion.

The doctor added that from the nature of an injury that he found that he thought that the interference might have been self-induced.

The police said that they carried out inquiries but found no one who might be suspected of having carried out the interference.

The coroner then recorded a verdict stating that Hannah Hudson died from blood poisoning due to a self-induced abortion.

Carl Winnberg

Age: unknown

Sex: male

Date: 29 May 1943

Place: Wartling Road, Pevensey

Carl Winnberg was run over.

He was found seriously injured on the Wartling Road in Pevensey around midnight on 28 May 1943 and was taken to the Princess Alice Hospital where he died the following day, 29 May 1943.

He had multiple injuries and it was thought that a very heavy vehicle must have passed over him.

He was found by the driver and passengers of a 10hp Hillman saloon car who said that they passed him on the road and when they went back to him, they found him already injured.

At his inquest the coroner said that there was no evidence to show that the 10hp Hillman had been the vehicle responsible for causing his injuries and the coroner concluded that he had been runover by an unknown vehicle and returned an open verdict.

Carl Winnberg was a Canadian soldier.

Richard Ballinger

Age: 87

Sex: male

Date: 29 May 1943

Place: Great West Road, Brentford

Richard Ballinger was knocked down on the Great West Road by a vehicle that didn't stop.

He was knocked down by the vehicle on the Great West Road in a black-out in December 1942, but after a period at home he was admitted to West Middlesex Hospital suffering from an abscess in the groin, where he stayed for three weeks, making a full recovery. However, on 15 May 1943 he was sent back to the hospital on his doctor's advice and later died.

At his inquest, the pathologist said that he could find no trace of injury but said that his brain was congested and that there was evidence of pneumonia which he said was the cause of death following a collection of pus that was set up by his fall.

It had been a dark and wet night and Richard Ballinger said that he had been crossing the road when something hit him, however, he said that he didn't see what it was.

An open verdict was returned.

He had lived at 48 Orchard Road in Brentford and was a retired painter.

He was buried in Ealing Cemetery on 26 May 1943.

Doris Hounslow

Age: 22

Sex: female

Date: 9 May 1943

Place: 24 Stanley Road, Tunbridge Wells

Doris Hounslow died from a septic abortion.

She died in hospital on the 9 May 1943.

She was married to a man serving in the army and had two children, a 2-year-old boy and a 14-month old girl.

At her inquest it was heard that her husband had come home just after Christmas.

An aunt of Doris Hounslow said that in early March 1943 Doris Hounslow asked her to go to the hospital with her to have two teeth extracted but that on the morning they were due to go Doris Hounslow complained of feeling unwell and when a doctor was later called for her he advised her to go to the hospital. The aunt said that at no time did

Doris Hounslow mention to her that she had been in a certain condition or that she had done anything to avert that.

It was noted that she had been quite happy and comfortable with her children.

Another aunt said that when she went to visit Doris Hounslow in hospital, Doris Hounslow told her that she had taken a number of Beecham's pills.

A doctor at the hospital said that Doris Hounslow told her that on 5 March 1943 she had had a sudden and severe haemorrhage and also admitted taking 100 Beecham's pills over three days.

She said that her condition was due to a partial abortion and that she was given appropriate treatment and seemed to improve after admission, but later became worse and died on 9 May 1943.

The doctor said that she found no evidence of any instrumental interference and concluded that her death was due to pneumonia and peritonitis following an abortion.

Baby

Age: 0

Sex: male

Date: 7 May 1943

Place: Grand Union Canal, Northampton

The body of a newly-born child was found in the Grand Union Canal between Northampton and Hunsbury Hill.

It was thought that the child had been dead for three months and the post-mortem concluded that there was no evidence to show that the child had been born alive.

The post-mortem also stated that there was no evidence of violence on the child's body and that the child had had no skilled attention at birth.

Israel Benjamin

Age: 45

Sex: male

Date: 25 Apr 1943

Place: Kentish Town Railway Station

Israel Benjamin died after falling out of a railway carriage shortly after it left Kentish Town Railway Station at 10.16am on 24 April 1943.

His 44-year-old brother was tried for his murder but acquitted.

After Israel Benjamin fell from the train and was found he said that his brother had pushed him out in a row over a will which his brother had benefitted from.

Their father had died on 18 April 1943 leaving a will that was dated 31 March 1943. The brother, who was one of the executors, was left with the house, 169 Watford Road in Harrow, along with the contents and the residue, apart from a small legacy which was divided equally between six other children.

The train that they had been on was a LMS train travelling from Broad Gate to Wembley. It had stopped shortly after leaving Kentish Town West station at 10.16am, travelling to Gospel Oak about three quarters of a mile out after the brother pulled the communication cord. After the brother pulled the communication cord, the train guard said that he looked out and saw that a carriage door was open and said that when he got out to look the brother looked out of the open door and said that a man had fallen out. The train guard said that he asked the brother if he had seen Israel Benjamin fall out and he said that he had not and that he had been asleep in the opposite corner and that he didn't know anything until he heard a bang, after which he pulled the emergency cord.

When the train guard asked the brother if he knew Israel Benjamin he said 'No'. They then walked along the the line until they got to Israel Benjamin. His brother then said, 'He's dead' and the train guard replied, 'He looks it'. They were then joined by the train driver who the brother also told that he didn't know Israel Benjamin. When the train driver asked the brother if he knew the injured man, the brother said, 'No. He was in the same compartment as me and I was dozing. I heard a thud and saw he was missing so I pulled the communication cord'.

The train guard said that he then made certain arrangements for the safety of the train and then returned to where Israel Benjamin was lying and that to his surprise Israel Benjamin spoke to him. The train guard said that the train driver then joined him, and Israel Benjamin continued to talk and told them that the other man was his brother and that he had pushed him out of the carriage. He said Israel Benjamin said, 'He tried to rob me, my brother', and when the train guard asked Israel Benjamin who his brother was, Israel Benjamin said, 'The man in the coach with me'.

The train guard said that he then approached the brother and said, 'Did you say you did not know him?', and said that the brother replied, 'I don't know him'. The train guard said that he then said, 'You had better come back. He is speaking', and said that the brother asked, 'Isn't he dead', and the train guard said that he said, 'No, he is very much alive, and he says he is your brother'.

When they went back they were joined by a police inspector and a sergeant and the police inspector said to Israel Benjamin, 'Do you believe you are dying?', and said that Israel Benjamin replied, 'I am'. Israel Benjamin then made certain statements that the inspector took down in his note book. During his statement he said, 'He took everything away from me. When the will was read my brother took the lot. We quarrelled over the will in the train. He said, 'You will not get anything. You have got to work'. I said, 'I want a half share'. He called me no good. He got me by the neck and pushed me out'.

The brother then said, 'Was not I asleep in the corner?' to which Israel Benjamin replied, 'No, you quarrelled and pushed me out'.

However, Israel Benjamin was unable to sign the statement and was removed by ambulance to Hampstead General Hospital but died before he arrived.

When the brother was taken to the police station the inspector said to him, 'You know what your brother said?' and the brother said, 'All I know is that he is the biggest liar out'.

A while later when the brother was asked to explain what he knew of the matter he said, 'A man got out of our compartment at Kentish Town West. My brother was sitting opposite me, the train moved off and I fell asleep. I don't know what happened. I heard the carriage door bang, found that my brother had gone and pulled the cord. We had not quarrelled, we were friendly'.

At 7.30pm that evening, 25 April 1943, the police arrested the brother for the murder of Israel Benjamin and when he was asked whether he understood, he said, 'I understand', and then said, 'I am not guilty'.

At the police-court, the prosecution said, 'The case rests almost entirely upon the dying declaration of Israel Benjamin. Apart from that the conduct of the accused does need some explanation. It is difficult to understand why, when he was first questioned by the guard and the train driver, he should have denied any knowledge of who deceased was. His story was that after leaving Kentish Town West station he had fallen asleep, but the train had travelled only 230 yards'.

The brother later said in evidence that Israel Benjamin was a waster and that he had caused him a good deal of expense and had opened the door of the carriage and had said, 'I am going to do myself in'.

Israel Benjamin's family doctor also said that Israel Benjamin was neurotic and had delusions that he suffered from diabetes and had a growth on the brain, which he said were both without foundation.

The post-mortem revealed that Israel Benjamin had all his ribs fractured, his spine fractured, his left arm fractured and had a depressed fracture of the skull although there was no sign of injury to the brain. The pathologist noted that there was no bruising to his throat and that death was due to shock following multiple crushing injuries.

The police said that they thought that in all probability that the extensive injuries that Israel Benjamin had received were caused by him being thrown between the moving train and the span girder in the middle of the permanent way, the clearance of which was ten inches.

When the carriage door was examined it was found to have had a 'Kays Slamb' type lock and safety catch with a short inside lever handle. The lock was found to have been in perfect condition and it was noted that to open the door from the inside, that it was necessary to fully depress the inside lever handle and hold it down until the door was past the safety catch, the idea being to prevent the door opening if the lever was accidently touched. It was further added that the tongue slot on the door standing pillar was fitted two inches from the safety catch which meant that it was possible to open the door two inches before being stopped by the safety catch. It was further noted that the inside lever handle was two and a half inches long.

The police also spoke to the two people that had been travelling in the next compartment of the train, but neither of them said they had heard any sound of a quarrel and could not assist.

However, the police said that they were unable to identify the third man that the brother said had been in their compartment and who had got out at Kentish Town West station.

The jury retired for two minutes before returning their verdict.

Bella

Age: 35

Sex: female

Date: 18 Apr 1943

Place: Hagley Woods, Wychbury Hill, Hereford and Worcester

The body of a woman was found in a tree by poachers.

The woman's identity was never determined but she was later named Belladonna and Bella.

She was found in a Witch Elm tree in Hagley Wood on the Hagley Estate in Hereford and Worcester by four boys who were bird-nesting at about midday on Sunday 18 April 1943. One of the boys said that he left the others and went to the stump of an old elm and that when he looked in he saw a skull. He said that he then called his other friends over and that they then raked out the skull with a stick and then put it back in. When they got back home one of the boys mentioned the find to his father who then called the police.

When a policeman went to the scene he said that the tree was about 35 yards from a lane that was accessible to motor traffic and which was used a good deal by courting couples.

The police noted that there had been a gipsy camp there two or three years earlier.

A professor with the West Midlands Forensic Science Laboratory said that he ruled out the possibility of suicide or accident. He said that he went to the wood and had the tree trunk opened out and had the skeleton extracted and that when he was finally able to reconstruct the skeleton, he found it to be that of a woman probably aged about 35 years. He added that there was no evidence of violence on any of the bones. The woman was said to have had mousey hair and the remains of her clothing suggested that she had been wearing dark blue and mustard coloured clothes.

Her full description was given as aged between 25 and 40 years, most probably 35, five feet in height, light mousey brown hair, neither dyed not bleached and with a noticeable irregularity of the front teeth in the lower jaw. Her clothing was described as consisting of a dark blue and light khaki or mustard-coloured striped knitted woollen cardigan with cloth-covered buttons, and belt of slightly lighter shade of blue, blue stripe in cardigan itself, light khaki or mustard-coloured woollen cloth skirt, with side patent fastening and blue crepe-soled shoes size 5 1/2. The general quality of her garments was described as being poor and it was thought that she had not been wearing stockings.

A wedding ring was also found with her remains with the words 'Rolled gold' stamped inside.

However, he said that he found part of a garment stuffed deep into the cavity of her mouth and said that that might have been her cause of death.

He said that he thought that her body had been in the tree for at least 18 months and probably much longer. He added that he could not imagine anyone getting into the tree voluntarily, stating that the aperture of the tree hollow came down from 24 inches to 17 inches. and he concluded that he thought that the woman had been killed within a short distance of the tree and while her body was still warm that she was put into the tree. He also noted that she might have been killed a greater distance away and then brought to the scene by car. He said that he was certain that her body had not been stiff when she was pushed into the tree.

The police said that they had no clues regarding anyone's involvement in the affair. They also said that it seemed quite definite that the woman was not of the locality and their investigations revealed no one that could remember seeing a woman matching the description of the dead woman at any time.

The police said that they did find a pair of shoes in the hollow tree trunk and it was thought that they might have aided in her identification.

Hagley was described as a rural spot that was within easy reach of Birmingham and the Black Country and to have attracted many visitors during the summer who went there by road, hiking, cycling or by bus. It was reported that when petrol was available for pleasure that people went to the woods in large numbers by motorcar, picnicking there and sometimes camping on the other side of the road from the wood.

It was also noted that evacuees also drifted there in considerable numbers during the lively enemy air activity over Birmingham early in the war.

Hagley Wood itself was accessible only by foot. The lane that ran up to it, described as a narrow winding lane, little more than a cart-track, ran beside the wood and was described as being easily negotiable by car up to the point where a five-barred gate afforded entrance to the wood. However, it was noted that the gate itself was locked. It was said that if the body had been taken by car that it would have had to have been carried some distance along a woodland path and then through some undergrowth before reaching the elm tree.

It was further noted that the risk of discovery in taking the body there by car during the day would be great and as such, if it had been taken by car, then it was probably done at night.

It was also noted that if the body had been brought by car to the wood then the murderer would have had to have known of the existence of the tree.

At her inquest a verdict of murder by some person or persons unknown was returned.

The mystery of her death took on a number of folkloresque theories including it being a black magic execution and that she was a German spy that had been spying for the Luftwaffe.

Baby

Age: 0

Sex: female

Date: 15 Apr 1943

Place: Chester General Station, Chester

The body of a newly born female child was found in a third class compartment of a train at Chester General Station.

The body was found in a third-class compartment after it arrived at the station at about 8am, on 15 April 1943 by a carriage cleaner.

The carriage cleaner, who was employed by the LMS Railway Company at Chester Station said that on the morning of 15 April 1943 she had been on duty on platform 7 when the train arrived from Whitchurch at 8.05am. She said that she walked along the platform and saw a green carrier bag in a third-class compartment, placed behind a steam cylinder. She said that she then went into the compartment and took the bag, intending to take it to the Lost Property Office but instead handed it to an inside cleaner who took it to the foreman and when they opened the bag they saw the head of the child.

The pathologist that carried out the post-mortem said that the child had had a separate existence and that the cause of death was lack of attention at birth. He noted that the child had a large wound across the front of its face which was due largely to heat but said that the wound was inflicted after death.

The coroner returned an open verdict.

Maurice Stuart Horner

Age: 49

Sex: male

Date: 5 Apr 1943

Place: 6 Maurice Walk, Finchley

Maurice Stuart Horner was found dead in his home in Finchley.

He died from head injuries.

He was the technical editor of Commercial Motor.

It was thought that a Canadian soldier was responsible for his death and the police interviewed over 100 Canadian soldiers.

A verdict of murder against a person or persons unknown was returned. The verdict stated that 'Maurice Stuart Horner, aged 49 years, died on the 5th April 1943, from coma and haemorrhage resulting from fracture of the skull, caused on 2nd April 1943, at Number 6 Maurice Walk, Finchley, N2, when he was struck on the head by some person or persons unknown; further that the cause of such death was murder by some person or persons unknown'.

Number 6 Maurice Walk in Finchley, N2, was a double fronted detached house. On the ground floor there was a large lounge, a dining room and a kitchen. On the first floor there was a bedroom over the lounge in which the family slept, a spare bedroom over the dining room in which guests slept, a small bedroom over the kitchen which was not used, and a small box room over the downstairs hall. There was a front and a back garden, and on one side of the house there was a garage and on the other, the front and back gardens adjoined. The houses to either side were some distance away and there were also houses on the opposite side of the street. The house itself was easily accessible by bus and tube and was in the heart of a very quiet residential neighbourhood. It was noted that the house would normally be void of traffic other than tradesmen's' vehicles and the cars of residents or visitors. It was further noted that neither the pavement or roadway was made up and that in the still of the night it would have been easy to hear anyone passing up and down the street.

Maurice Horner had married on 4 February 1931, and according to his wife, their relationship had been perfectly normal, and they had never had any serious disagreements, although she noted that at times they slept in separate beds. They had no children.

Maurice Horner's wife noted that Maurice Horner had met strange men in the past and brought them home and that they had slept the night in the spare room. However, she added that she too had also brought friends home in the past who had also stayed the night.

Maurice Horner's wife was an auxiliary ambulance driver under the LCC doing her duty at Hampstead. Her hours of duty were twenty-four hours on and twenty four hours off, commencing at 9am and as such on alternate nights she would be on duty and not get back home until after she reported off duty at 9am.

It was noted that it was customary for Maurice Horner on the nights that his wife was off duty for him to go straight home after leaving his office, usually arriving back home at about 6.30pm, although it was also noted that he sometimes worked late at the office. However, it was heard that on the nights that Maurice Horner's wife was working, Maurice Horner did not appear to be too anxious to get home early and would often call at public houses on the way home. As such, it was noted that on such nights, Maurice Horner had ample opportunity of taking home anyone he pleased, and that provided his guests left the house before his wife came home the following morning, that there was little likelihood of her knowing if he had so wished to keep it from her.

It was found that Maurice Horner would sometimes cycle to and from business, but that sometimes he would travel by trolleybus and on other days he would walk a considerable part of the distance. The police stated that they found that on the evenings that his wife was on duty, Maurice Horner would visit public houses in the vicinity of his business, Kings Cross, Highbury, Highgate and East Finchley, depending on his method of journeying home that particular evening.

Maurice Horner had been employed as the technical editor with Commercial Motor at

Temple Press Ltd, Bowling Green Lane, EC1, and was regarded by all those associated with him as a very intelligent and efficient man who drank a fair amount of beer. However, it was noted that in spite of that, he kept a clear head and was often known, after a heavy drinking bout, to have returned to his office late in the evening and to have written highly technical articles for his periodical.

He was known as a 'hail fellow well let' type and as being quick to make acquaintances, although noted as being inclined to become argumentative, especially after a few drinks.

A freelance journalist that knew Maurice Horner, who refused to make a written statement, said that in 1929 he had been with Temple Press when he had first met Maurice Horner. He said that at that time Maurice Horner had liked his beer and had been very fond of women, and said that when Maurice Horner married in 1931, he hoped that he would settle down. He said that he believed that Maurice Horner had been faithful to his wife until the beginning of the war when he said that Maurice Horner told him that he was no longer interested in women, but only boys. The freelance journalist said that Maurice Horner was quite frank about it and would often tell him of the good times that he had had with boys. The freelance journalist added that he thought that Maurice Horner's wife knew of Maurice Horner's homosexual tendencies.

In September 1940, Maurice Horner became a member of the 12th Company, 20th Battalion, Middlesex Home Guard, and held the rank of lance corporal and was attached to the Intelligence Section. The headquarters of the Company was based in Cyprus Road in Finchley, which was some distance, about three quarters of a mile, from Maurice Walk. It was located at The Five Bells Public House in East End Road, East Finchley, and the section met three evenings a week. His commanding officer said that Maurice Horner's conduct was exceptional and said that he was exceedingly popular with everyone. However, the Captain did say that after hearing of Maurice Horner's association with a younger member of the Home Guard he transferred Maurice Horner to another Home Guard Section where there were no young members and also compelled the other party, the younger man, to resign.

The licensee of The Five Bells Public House said that he knew Maurice Horner well, both as a customer as well as a member of the

Home Guard. He said that Maurice Horner was a good natured individual, but noted that he had for some time been fond of the company of young men, in particular a young man who was also in the Home Guard Company and he said that Maurice Horner would leave his other home guard colleagues to join the younger man at the public house, which was seen as a very odd association in view of the difference in their ages and intelligence. It was after hearing of those associations that the Captain of the Home Guard Company transferred Maurice Horner.

A man that lived at 5 Montpelier Road, N3, said that he had known Maurice Horner for about six years and that he usually met him in one or other of the local public houses in East Finchley. He said that apart from his association with the young man in the Home Guard unit, he would often see Maurice Horner with other men considerably younger than himself and added that Maurice Horner didn't appear to be the least bit interested in women, adding that in fact he had seen him leave the company of his wife in public houses and join the company of young men there. The man added that Maurice Horner would buy anyone a drink and would often get into conversations with strangers. He added that Maurice Horner was always willing to help anyone in difficulties.

The police interviewed many other people that knew Maurice Horner and who gave descriptions of his character and their suspicions, including a 23-year-old photographer who lived in Allandale Avenue, N3. The police noted that he was a personal friend of Maurice Horner and came from good parents, was well educated and good looking. The police said that although there was no evidence of anything unusual happening between them, they did note that the photographer had visited Maurice Horner's home many times and had been out with Maurice Horner in his car.

When the police examined Maurice Horner's movements, they found that he left his home soon after 9am on Thursday 1 April 1943 for business, with his wife leaving at about the same time for her twenty four hours duty at Hampstead, meaning that she was not expected back home until after about 10am the following morning, and as such the house was left unattended throughout the day.

Maurice Horner arrived at Temple Press Ltd in Bowling Green Lane, EC1 at about 10am after which he almost immediately went out in the firm's car with a photographer with the firm to Wembley, Willesden, Park Royal, Alperton and North Acton, on business, arriving back at the offices at about 4.15pm. Maurice Horner then stayed in the office until a little after 5pm when he said goodnight to his editor and left the building alone.

He was seen shortly after at about 6pm when he entered the saloon bar of the Montrose public house in Roman Way, Barnsbury, N7, at which time he was alone. He was a regular customer there and the assistant manager remembered serving him two ham rolls and three or four glasses of mild and bitter.

At around 7pm, a 21-year-old man came into the pub. He knew both Maurice Horner and the assistant manager there and stopped to speak to them. He said that Maurice Horner told him about being in Wembley on business that day by car and then told him that he was 'freelance' that evening as his wife was on night duty and tried to persuade the 21-year-old to go to his local, The Five Bells public house in Finchley with him.

However, the 21-year-old man refused the invitation and both the 21-year-old and the assistant manager at the Montrose public house said they saw Maurice Horner leave the pub alone at about 7.45pm.

Later that evening, the manager of the Apple Tree public house in Mount Pleasant, WC1, who said that he had known Maurice Horner as a customer for years, said that he had gone into the Adam and Eve public house in Euston Road at about 8.15pm and had seen Maurice Horner. However, he said that because he knew that it would have been difficult to have gotten away from Maurice Horner if he had seen him, he said that he left quickly without buying a drink and without Maurice Horner seeing him. He added that he did not notice whether Maurice Horner had been in anyone's company when he saw him, but said that he did appear to be sober.

A 42-year-old prostitute who lived in Duncan Terrace in Islington, N1, said that she had been standing outside Warren Street Tube Station in Tottenham Court Road, at about 9.30pm, which was not far from the Adam and Eve public house, when she said that a man that she was positive was Maurice Horner said something to her about her looking lonely. She said that he then asked her where she was going and that when she told him that 'she was out for business', he offered her 10/-. She said that she accepted the money and that they then went to Mortimer Market, close to where they met, where she said Maurice Horner felt her breasts from the outside of her clothing. However. other than that, she said that nothing untoward happened, but did say that she could feel his erect person pushing against her. She said that afterwards they walked back into Tottenham Court Road, where she said he left her at about 10.10pm and headed off down Tottenham Court Road in the direction of Goodge Street.

A man that was in the Fitzroy Tavern public house in Windmill Street, W1, at about 8pm on 1 April 1943, said that he was positive that he saw Maurice Horner there at about 10pm. He said that he saw him at the bar and that as far as he could remember, he saw Maurice Horner buy drinks for a soldier, and airman and a girl that was with the airman. However, he noted that the soldier, airman and the girl were not in his company and that after buying the drinks, Maurice Horner left them. The man, whose wife worked in the pub as a barmaid, said that he thought that Maurice Horner had had sufficient to drink and said to him, 'Don't you think you have had enough old man!' and said that Maurice Horner replied, 'I am going in a minute'. The man said that he saw Maurice Horner leave the pub shortly afterwards.

It was noted that the sighting of Maurice Horner in the Fitzroy Tavern was the last known sighting of him.

The woman that lived at 1 Hilltop, Finchley, whose garden adjoined that of 6 Maurice Walk, said that she had gone to bed at about 12.30am on 2 April 1943 and that at about 12.45am that morning, she heard sounds of running footsteps and the sound of scuffling. She said that she was not sure where the sounds came from, the front or the back, and said that she didn't get out of bed to look, but that she did mention it to her husband.

A daily help, who worked at 6 Maurice Walk on Mondays, Wednesdays and Fridays of each week, and who had a set of keys to the front door of his house, having worked for him for six years, said that she went to 6 Maurice Walk at about 9.30am on Friday 2 April 1943 and opened the front door with her key. She said that just inside the front door, in the hall, she saw a pool of blood and a broken kitchen chair. She said that she then saw Maurice Horner's slippers, his pipe, driving licence, matches, glasses and two notebooks, on the bottom stair and said that she then put the items, with the exception of the slippers, on the chest of drawers in the hall. She said that she then went into the kitchen, which was blacked-out, but said that she could not get the electric light to switch on. She said that she then went upstairs to the bedroom that Maurice Horner and his wife slept in and switched on the electric light there and saw Maurice Horner lying in bed with a towel round his head. She said that Maurice Horner was dressed in his pyjamas and that the towel and his bedclothes were covered in blood. She said that the room was also blacked out and that she then asked Maurice Horner, 'Whatever happened?' and said that Maurice Horner replied, 'A Canadian soldier did this'. She said that she then asked him 'How did he come here?' and said that Maurice Horner replied, 'I walked home from East Finchley Tube Station with him for a cup of tea. When we got home, I made some tea. The soldier then started to set into me. I lost consciousness and I woke up cold'.

The daily help said that she then went into the kitchen and made Maurice Horner a weak cup of tea and took it back up to him and then suggested calling for a doctor but said that Maurice Horner told her not to, and asked her to wait until his wife had got home. The daily help said that she then suggested that she should at least call the police, but said that Maurice Horner again asked her not to, asking her to wait until his wife returned.

When the daily help went back into the kitchen and took down the blackout shutters she then saw the disorder there. She said the electric light bulb and shade were broken, there was another broken kitchen chair as well as a broken saucer. She said that there were plates, a knife, a fork, and a spoon in a bowl of water in the sink, on top of which there was an empty casserole dish. She added that the water appeared to be coloured with blood. She said that there were also two cups and a teapot overturned on the kitchen table and two drinking glasses were also on the table, one half full of water and the other empty and that she formed the opinion that two people had had a meal.

The daily help said that the back door was locked from the inside when she arrived and said that no one could have left the house by that door.

She said that the broken chair that she found just inside the front door was usually kept in the kitchen.

She also said that the notebooks, driving licence, matches, pipe, tobacco pouch and spectacles that she found on the bottom stair in the hall were in a row as though they had been placed that way by someone.

She said that she saw blood on the carpets in the lounge and a blood covered handkerchief on the carpet there and noted that the blackout had also not been removed in the lounge. She said that she also saw blood on the stairs.

She said that the bedclothes on the bed in the spare room which was generally used by guests were partly turned back and that there were a pair of folded pyjamas on the pillow and that it didn't look like anyone had slept in the bed the previous night. She noted also that the blackout was not drawn in that room.

After looking about the daily help then began to clear up the mess, washing up the cups, picking up the pieces of broken chairs and putting them in the garden and washing away some of the blood on the kitchen floor as well as the pool of blood just inside the front door.

It was in the midst of clearing up that Maurice Horner's wife came home at about 10.20am on 2 April 1943. When she got home the front door was open and she was immediately told what had happened by the daily help after which she told the daily help to immediately cease clearing up and to leave everything alone.

Maurice Horner's wife then went up to see Maurice Horner who was still in bed with the towel round his head. She said that she called him by name and that he replied, 'Hello'. She said that she then made a quick examination, felt his pulse and noticed that he was breathing alright and then went back downstairs and telephoned for the doctor and for the police.

Maurice Horner's wife said that she then went back upstairs and asked Maurice Horner how long he had been lying there, and said that he told her, 'Since about twelve'.

There was a telephone at the side of the bed and the daily help was in the room when Maurice Horner used the phone and dialled a number. She said that she held the receiver to his ear for him and said that he spoke coherently.

The assistant editor of the Temple Press Ltd was in his office just before 10am on 2 April 1943 when he received a telephone call from Maurice Horner, the call that the daily help had referred to and had helped Maurice Horner make. He said that he didn't know who it was at first, as he appeared dazed, but when Maurice Horner told him that he would not be able to keep his business appointment that morning he realised who he was speaking to. He said that when Maurice Horner called, Maurice Horner said, 'Good morning old boy' and that he then said, 'Good morning old chap'. The assistant editor said that Maurice Horner then went on to tell him that he was not going to be able to keep an important business appointment that morning and then told him that he had a gash on his head as a result of taking a Canadian soldier home for a cup of tea. The assistant editor said that Maurice Horner also mentioned that he had been unconscious or asleep and that when he woke up the Canadian soldier had disappeared.

A doctor arrived at 6 Maurice Walk at about 10.30am. He said that when he arrived, he found Maurice Horner's head and face a mass of contusion and blood. He said that he had a deep gash in his scalp and appeared to have a fractured skull and that he made arrangements by telephone for an ambulance to take him immediately to the University College Hospital in Gower Street.

The doctor said that in his opinion, the injuries that he saw could have been made by blows from the broken chairs.

The police were called at 10.42am by Maurice Horner's wife who said that she had just returned home and found Maurice Horner in bed suffering from injuries and that the house was in disorder. The message was repeated to Finchley police station and police arrived at 6 Maurice Walk at about 11am on 2 April 1943. They said that just as they arrived, they saw Maurice Horner being carried into a waiting ambulance to be taken to the University College Hospital.

When the police arrived, they gave instructions that nothing was to be touched. When the police found that the daily help had moved a number of things, she was told to replace them at once whilst the places where she had found them was fresh in her mind, which she did with gloved hands.

The police then examined the house and found in addition to what the daily help had spoken of, bloodstains on the larder and cupboard doors in the kitchen and on the kitchen floor leading into the hall. They also found marks on the wall in the hall leading from the kitchen to the lounge that appeared to have been made by someone with their elbow as they staggered along.

They also found that the carpet on the lower stairs was also bloodstained.

The police also found a large bloodstain on the wall just inside the front door, and between that door and the dining room door they found two small stains on the wall in the angle between the front door and the door to the lounge.

Apart from the large pool of blood on the carpet in front of the sofa in the lounge, the police found stains on the wall immediately below the bay window on the far side of the room. They said that the rug in front of the fireplace, close to the sofa, was also disarranged.

When the police searched Maurice Horner's bedroom, they found his collar, tie and handkerchief, all of which were bloodstained, on a chest of drawers. His suit and shirt were on a chair near the chest, and they appeared to have been placed there in the normal way. The police also found blood stains on the wall immediately behind the chair, four feet from the floor.

The police said that they found no evidence of the house having been forcibly entered and were of the opinion that Maurice Horner and another person had been in the house since Maurice Horner and his wife had left the house the previous morning.

When Maurice Horner was taken to hospital, the police arranged for a CID officer to be at his bedside at the hospital.

When Maurice Horner was admitted to the University College Hospital at about noon on 2 April 1943, a doctor who saw him said that he was conscious and able to answer questions coherently, but drowsily. The doctor said that when he asked Maurice Horner what had happened, Maurice Horner said that he had met a Canadian soldier in the tube going from Goodge Street to East Finchley and that he had invited him back to his house for tea. He said that after they got back to his house, the Canadian soldier struck him on the head with a chair as he was making the tea. He said that he tried to reason with the soldier but finally collapsed on the floor, bleeding profusely from the head. He said that the Canadian soldier then left and that he then managed to put himself to bed where he was found by his charlady the following morning. He added that he didn't know whether anything had been stolen and said that the attack took place around midnight.

At 1pm on 2 April 1943 Maurice Horner was asleep, and the police determined to get more information out of Maurice Horner. The doctor said that it would be some time before he could make a written statement and it was considered that because of the possible motive behind Maurice Horner's invitation to the Canadian soldier to come back to his house, that he might not tell the truth to the police and so it was agreed that the doctor would ask him some pre-arranged questions and that the presence of the police would be kept from him.

Maurice Horner later opened his eyes shortly after 2pm and the doctor asked him some questions:

Question: Where had you been yesterday?

Answer: I had been out of the office all day and had been to Alperton. I had no dinner.

Question: What time did you leave the office and where did you go?

Answer: I think I left about 5.30pm and went to the Montrose public house in Roman Way, Barnsbury. I had two ham rolls.

Question: Where did you go then?

Answer: I walked down to the Cale and got a bus to Kings Cross. I walked along towards Tottenham Court Road.

At that moment, Maurice Horner vomited and had a rest before continuing.

Question: Where did you meet the soldier?

Answer: He was on the platform. We went to East Finchley and walked through the passage to Edmunds Walk, over Deansway into Brim Hill. There were some other people at the station.

Question: What was the soldier's name and what did he look like?

Answer: He was shorter than me. He had dark hair and was rather good looking. He said he was a private in the artillery and spoke of the University at Winnipeg. He said he had been to Oxford and ran it down.

Question: Was the soldier on leave and where was he stationed?

Answer: I thought he was on leave.

Question: Are you sure he was a private?

Answer: He told me he had been a sergeant but had gone back to a private.

Question: Had you any money on you?

Answer: I think about 30/-.

Maurice Horner then became exhausted and went to sleep.

Soon after, a surgeon came in and determined that an immediate operation was required, and Maurice Horner was prepared and at 3.45pm the operation was started and it terminated at 6.30pm.

Maurice Horner was described as being in a stable state after the operation but was not able to speak.

The following day at about 5.30am, Maurice Horner woke up and began to mumble to the detective that was by his bed, and over the following hour, he made the following disjointed sentences:

- I went home, made some tea.
- His name was Rex.
- I don't know what happened, blows just seemed to rain on my head from everywhere.
- He was a private.
- Battledress.
- Dark hair, nice looking chap.
- I think he was from Winnipeg, Canada.
- He was in the REME.
- Not very pronounced Canadian.
- Between 35 and 40 years.

Maurice Horner then lost consciousness again and said nothing further.

Maurice Horner's condition then gradually deteriorated and on the evening of 4 April 1943, the surgeon in charge thought that it was advisable to open up his wound again and another operation was performed that evening.

Maurice Horner was said to have derived some relief from the second operation, but was deeply comatosed by the afternoon of 5 April 1943.

However, he died at 8.15pm on 5 April 1943 without saying anything further.

After Maurice Horner's death, the police stated that they had very little in the way of evidence to present in court, the only evidence they had being that of the condition of the house given by the daily help, Maurice Horner's wife and the police that arrived at the scene, that property had been stolen, the medical evidence regarding the cause of death and finger impressions that were found that were thought belonged to the person that committed the offence.

However, the police added that, provided Maurice Horner had told the truth, that they had some material to work on, based on his statements regarding the Canadian soldier.

The police stated that if they accepted what Maurice Horner tod them as true, then he met a man with the following description: 'A

Canadian soldier, between 35 and 40 years of age, shorter than himself (Maurice Horner was 5ft 9in in height), dark hair, good looking, in battle dress, attached to the Artillery or REME, not very pronounced Canadian accent, who was thought to be on leave at the time, who spoke of the University at Winnipeg, had been to Oxford and ran it down and had at one time been a sergeant and had been demoted to a private'.

When the police reconstructed the apparent course of events, they said that it appeared that Maurice Horner had met the Canadian soldier on the evening of 1 April 1943 on the platform of Goodge Street underground station. It was thought that they then both went by train to East Finchley station and that, as described by Maurice Horner, they then took the most direct route from the station to 6 Maurice Walk, Finchley. The police said that they thought they probably arrived at 6 Maurice Walk soon after 11.30pm when they both shared the meal that Maurice Horner's wife had left prepared on the kitchen table for him in the usual way. The police noted that they had evidence of that as the daily help said that she had found two cups and a teapot, the empty casserole dish and two drinking glasses, one with water in it, when she entered on the morning of 2 April 1943.

The police reconstruction of the apparent course of events then stated that Maurice Horner then suddenly spoke of being struck on the head with a chair and that blows just seemed to rain on his head from everywhere. Maurice Horner was noted as having then to tried to reason with the soldier, but without avail, and to have then collapsed. The police stated that they thought that the struggle probably finished in the hall near the front door just inside of which the daily help said she found one of the broken kitchen chairs and a large pool of blood. The police stated that it then appeared that the Canadian soldier then rifled through Maurice Horner's pockets whilst he was on the floor unconscious. It was thought that the Canadian soldier then stole Maurice Horner's wallet, his cigarette case and cigarette lighter and placed the things that he didn't want, the pipe and matches etc, on the bottom stair near him, and then made his escape by the front door, which was found closed by the daily help when she arrived.

The police concluded that based on the apparent facts, that the assault took place at about midnight and that it was no doubt the assailant that the neighbour had heard at about 12.45am as he fled the house.

The police then stated that when Maurice Horner later regained consciousness, that he said that he found the soldier had gone and that whilst bleeding profusely from his head injuries, he had no doubt put his hands to his head and as a result they had become covered in blood. It was thought that he had then dragged himself to his feet and whilst doing so had made the blood marks on the hall wall and had then made his way into the lounge. It was noted that the outer handle of the lounge door was found to have blood on it, caused when he opened it, and it was thought that as he went in that he tripped over the rug in front of the fire which was found to be disarranged, and then fallen to the floor with his head near the sofa where a large pool of blood and the blood stained handkerchief were found.

It was thought that he had not been able to switch on the electric light in the lounge on as the room had not been blacked out. It was thought that he probably lost consciousness for a while and that when he regained consciousness , he drew himself up with the aid of the sofa to his feet and then made his way back into the hall by way of the bay window beneath which there were further bloodstains. It was thought that when he had reached the hall that he had then probably dragged himself up the stairs, at which point his slippers dropped off his feet, and that he helped himself up the stairs by holding the wall upon which other bloodstains were found.

The police said that they thought that when he reached his bedroom he then put his bloodstained collar and tie on the chest of drawers and took off his suit and shirt and put them on the back of a chair, found a towel in the bedroom which he then wrapped around his head and then put on his pyjamas on and went to bed.

The police said that they thought that he remained in that position until his daily help arrived and found him, about nine hours after the assault.

The police report stated that if that assumption of events was correct, that the police probably arrived at the scene probably between ten and eleven hours after the assailant had left the house.

The police said that assuming that Maurice Horner had told the truth, that they did not think that Maurice Horner had met the Canadian soldier before 1 April 1943. The police noted that as the technical editor of the Commercial Motor that he would have been deeply interested in a soldier who had knowledge of the mechanisms of tanks and like army vehicles, and that a Canadian soldier attached to the REME would have been able to converse on those subjects with him and that that might have been his motive in bringing him back to his house.

However, the police noted that in view of Maurice Horner's past association with young men, that the soldiers knowledge of vehicles was not the main reason for inviting a 'nice looking chap' back to his house late at night for a cup of tea knowing that there would be no one else at home. The police suggested that whilst Maurice Horner had been making a cup of tea after they had had a meal that they were of the opinion that Maurice Horner made certain suggestions to which the soldier took a strong objection and that in his rage he punished Maurice Horner more severely than he had at first intended. The police reported noted that there was no doubt that the killer had also robbed Maurice Horner, but stated that they thought that the robbery was secondary to the assault and that it was not in his mind at the time that he accepted Maurice Horner's invitation back to his house.

The police later made house to house enquiries in Maurice Walk and the surrounding streets but found nothing to help the case other than the information received from the woman at 1 Hilltop who heard the man running away.

When the police visited 6 Maurice Walk on 2 April 1943 at about 2.15pm, they took fingerprints from several items, including two impressions on two pieces of one of the broken chairs and on a saucer found in the kitchen. When fingerprints of all the people known to have been in the house were also taken for purposes of elimination, the impression on the saucer was found to have belonged to Maurice Horner's wife whilst one of the impressions found on the broken chair was also found to have been hers. However, the police stated that the third impression from one of the broken chairs, which was the clearest impression of all, belonged to no one who could be identified. It was then compared to the fingerprints of all Canadian soldiers who had been arrested previously, but no matches were found.

The police were informed that Maurice Horner's wallet and 30/- were missing at 8.35pm on 2 April 1943.

At 9.10pm on 2 April 1943 an SS message was sent to SD Inspectors asking for enquiries to be made of all-night reliefs as to whether any soldiers had asked directions on the previous night and also that 'persons stopped in the street register', were to be searched.

At 9.50pm on 2 April 1943, a telephone message was sent to the Information Room, circulating the vague description of the wanted man along with the description of the stolen wallet.

As a result of the SS message sent out, a statement was obtained from a police constable who was attached to Finchley Station. He said that at about 10pm on 1 April 1943, he had been posted to a police box situated at the junction of the North Circular Road and East End Road, which was about half a mile from Maurice Walk. The officer said that he had been outside the box at about 12.45am in the morning, which he said was a very dark time although his box had a light on it that could be seen from some distance, when a soldier came up to him. He said that judging from the soldier's footsteps that he thought that he had come from the direction of East End Road and said that the soldier came up to him and asked him, 'How can I get to the Beaver Club from here?'. The constable said that he replied, 'Go down the North Circular Road and turn left into Regents Park Road and through Golders Green'. The constable said that the soldier then asked what the time was and so he opened his police box door and went inside where it was light, noting that the soldier then came up to the door, and said that he told him that it was 12.45am.

The constable said that he then asked the soldier, 'Are you adrift mate?', and said that the soldier replied 'No, I've got an hour or so out. I've been out with a couple of birds and left it rather late'. The constable said that he didn't ask the soldier for his pass. He said that the soldier had the appearance of having been drinking and said that his face was flushed and his breathing rapid as if he had been running. The constable said that he didn't see the soldier's hands and said that he saw no marks of injury about the soldier's face.

He said that the soldier had dark brown untidy hair, was about 25 years of age, about

5ft 8in tall, had a swarthy complexion, was clean shaven, sharp featured, with a thin face, slim build and a shortish nose. He added that the soldier was dressed in khaki battle dress without an overcoat or cap and that he had seen the word 'Canada' on his shoulder. He also added that the soldier was a private. The constable said that he didn't see any other marks on his blouse to signify his unit but stated that he thought that he would be able to identify the man again. He said that when they left the police box and then directed the soldier who he said, on leaving said to him, 'If I see a car, I will stop him and get a lift'.

The police report stated that as a result of that statement from the police constable that they caused enquiries to be made at the Beaver Club, Canadian Club, United States Club and the Overseas League Club, but that no useful information was obtained from them.

The police also spoke to all the local air raid wardens in the Maurice Walk district, but none of them saw or heard anything.

The police also spoke to all the drivers and conductors of early morning bus and trolley bus routes within reasonable distance of Maurice Walk, but without success.

The police also spoke to the late night and early morning staff at the East Finchley, Finchley Central, Golders Green and Hampstead Tube Stations, who were on duty on 1 and 2 April 1943, but they could not assist. There was one ticket collector who had been working on the barrier at East Finchley station on the evening of 1 April 1943 who said that amongst the excess fares he collected between 11pm and midnight was one of sixpence. However, he could not remember who paid it and was not able to recollect seeing anyone that matched the description of Maurice Horner or the Canadian soldier.

The police also traced five regular travellers who alighted at East Finchley station nightly between 11pm and midnight, but although they were shown a photograph of Maurice Horner, they were unable to throw any light on his movements.

The police also visited all the public houses in East Finchley, but it was established that Maurice Horner had not been to any of them on 1 April 1943.

When the police questioned the office staff at Temple Press, they said that they had not seen Maurice Horner with any Canadian soldiers. When the police searched his desk carefully for clues, they found nothing to indicate that he had been corresponding with any Canadian soldiers. His 1943 diary showed the nights that Maurice Horner had been on Home Guard duty, but otherwise the only other entries were for business appointments and the pubs that he had visited.

The police traced the route that Maurice Horner was thought to have taken from the office to the West End, which resulted in them determining that he had visited the following pubs:

- Montrose public house, Roman Way, N7 from 6pm till 7.45pm.
- Adam and Eve public house, Euston Road, at 8.15pm.
- Fitzroy public house, Windmill Street, W1, just after 10pm.

The investigation also determined that he was well known at quite a number of other public houses en route.

The police also made contact with informants in public houses in and around the Tottenham Court Road district as well as making enquiries at Goodge Street underground station, but they were unable to find anyone that had seen Maurice Horner after he had left the Fitzroy public house after 10pm on 1 April 1943.

The police also made special enquiries with CID officers at hospitals to see if anyone matching the description of the Canadian soldier had sought medical attention or had been detained in hospital, but without any luck.

After Maurice Horner died on 5 April 1943, the police took possession of hair that was found on the back of his jacket as well as a sample of hair from a brush that Maurice Horner had used, and they were handed to a doctor at Hendon Laboratory. They also later sent him Maurice Horner's jacket, waistcoat, trousers and shirt that he had been wearing on the day he was attacked along with a sample of hair from his head and a sample of his blood.

When the doctor analysed the blood from Maurice Horner, he said that it was blood group A2 and said that the extensive blood staining on Maurice Horner's clothing was also blood group A2.

He also confirmed that the hairs found encrusted in a blood clot on the back of Maurice Horner's jacket, were similar to those found on the head of Maurice Horner.

Later, on 9 April 1943, Maurice Horner's wife told the police that she was also missing a cigarette case that Maurice Horner always carried with him, and a description of it was then sent to the Information Room asking for special enquiries at pawnbrokers etc to trace it.

On Sunday 11 April 1943, a road roller driver who lived in Pearscroft Road, Fulham, said that on 2 April 1943, at about 11.20am, he had found a cigarette case lying on the nearside of the grass verge on the North Circular Road. He said that he had not thought much about it at the time but said that he had been reading about the murder in his Sunday newspaper in which it mentioned the missing cigarette case and as a result he took it to the police station. The cigarette case had the initials MSH on it. He had found it whilst driving his roller along the North Circular Road near the junction of East End Road. He said that he had put it in his pocket with the intention of handing it into the police but forgot of its existence until he read about the murder later in his newspaper. The roller driver then took the police to the spot where he found it which was about seven yards behind a seat on the grass verge at the junction of the North Circular Road and Falloden Way in Finchley.

The cigarette case was then identified by Maurice Horner's wife.

When the police examined the cigarette case, they found finger impressions of the roller driver as well as his friends, who also handled it after the roller driver found it, but the police said that they were satisfied that they were no involved with Maurice Horner's murder.

The police report noted that the police box where the constable had said he had spoken to a Canadian soldier was only 600 yards from the place where the cigarette case was found, and said that they felt that they had every right therefore to assume that the soldier who the constable had spoken to at 12.45am on 2 April 1943, was the wanted man.

Maurice Horner's wife later informed the police on 13 April 1943 that Maurice Horner's petrol lighter was also missing, and the police sent a description of it along to the Information Room so that it could be included in their enquiries.

On 5 May 1943, Maurice Horner's wife told the police that she was missing a small horseshoe shaped magnet that had always been kept in the kitchen, and although she had only just missed it, she suspected that the killer had taken it.

The police noted that Maurice Horner had said that he had met the Canadian soldier at Goodge Street underground station. However, they said that it was not clear whether he had met him on the platform or in the train, and as such, they stated that it was possible that Maurice Horner might have met the soldier on the tube train and that if he did, then it was possible that the soldier might have been heading to Mill Hill East Station and making for Mill Hill Military Barracks there.

As such, the police made enquiries at the barracks at which the 1st Battalion REME was stationed. They said that all relevant records were examined and nothing useful could be determined. Their enquiries also showed that no one in the Canadian army had been attached to Mill Hill Barracks that year and also that there were no other military establishments in the North of London to which Canadian soldiers were attached that could be reasonably reached by anyone travelling on the Edgeware to Morden Line in a northerly direction from Goodge Street underground station.

The police also made enquiries into the young man that Maurice Horner had been friendly with in the Home Guard. However, at the time, he was in Africa and letters sent to Great Scotland Yard to make arrangements to interview him were not replied to. The police did however speak to the youth's mother who confirmed that her son had been friendly with Maurice Horner and said that he used to stay at Maurice Horner's house when his wife was on duty and that they would often go into the West End together. The police said that whilst the chance was slim, that there was the possibility that if Maurice Horner had known the Canadian soldier, then the youth might also have known him, but they were unable to question him on that matter.

The police said that every possible assistance was rendered to them by the Canadian Special Investigation Section of the Canadian Provost Corps in Henrietta Street, W and that they had been in constant touch with them. They added that since the murder, every Canadian soldier who had been arrested and who it was considered likely to have been responsible was interrogated. They said that the nominal roll of Canadian soldiers absent without leave, or who had been struck off strength as deserters or who had escaped military custody, published on 7 April 1943 and 12 May 1943, were also examined. They also examined records of those that had not returned to their units, but the police concluded that the man they were looking for was not amongst the information in their possession.

When the police considered the statement that Maurice Horner had made about the Canadian soldier being in the artillery and having been to Oxford and ran it down, they made enquiries at the War Diaries Department, Canadian Military Headquarters Records Office in Acton and were informed that after Dunkirk, the British and Canadian armies were exceptionally short of guns and that as a result the

Canadian Artillery units were split up, contrary to army procedures, and scattered all over the country. As such, the police said that it was possible that one of those small groups had been posted at or near Oxford, but that it was impossible to find out anything about those groups as no records of them existed. It was noted however, that at the time of the murder, no part of the Canadian army was in the Oxford area.

The police report noted that the only other link between the Canadian Army and Oxford was the University Short Educational Course that was run by the Canadian Legion War Services in St Georges Hill in Weybridge. The courses were one week in duration and were open to any member in the forces of the colonies or allies, at the individual's own expense and in their own time. The object of the courses were to give the students an insight into the general methods of education at British universities. They started in June 1942 and in January 1943 there was a break until April 1943. The police said that when they went to the course office they found that a total of 900 Canadian soldiers had attended the courses, but said that because they had no information that the man they were looking for held a commission, they excluded the commissioned officers which left a list of 480 Canadian soldiers of other ranks.

The police also learnt that there had been a liaison officer at Oxford who stood between the Canadians and the University Authorities. It was found that that liaison officer came into personal touch with all the Canadians who attended the courses. However, when they spoke to two men that had acted as liaison officers over the relevant period, they found that they were unable to link any of the Canadian that had been on the courses with the description of the Canadian soldier they were looking for.

The police also went to see the records at the Canadian Records Office in Acton where they were given access to all the files of the Canadian Army serving in England which included where the man was born, his full description, where he was educated, where he enlisted, when he arrived in the country, all the units that he had belonged to, dates on which he had taken leave and crimes. The police then sorted out the 480 names that they had from the course office and as a result identified 21 Canadian soldiers whose records fitted in some detail or another with the man that they were looking for. They then requested various police forces around the country, and they were all interrogated, but they were all cleared of suspicion.

The police then searched the Canadian Army records for anyone with the name Rex, which had been given by Maurice Horner. They also searched for anyone with a name of any sort that sounded like Rex.

They identified one soldier in the Canadian army with the name Rex, and when investigations were made, it was found that he had been in barracks with the CROO at Martinique Barracks in Bordon, Hampshire and that he had answered roll call at 10pm on 1 April 1943.

The police added that they found two men in the Canadian army with the surname Rech and five men with the surname Rix, but said that after enquiries were made, they were satisfied that none of them were responsible for the murder.

The police also made enquiries into the statement that Maurice Horner had made regarding the Canadian Soldier saying that he had been to the University at Winnipeg. They said that when they made enquiries, they found that the university referred to was probably Manitoba University and found that part of it had been taken over as an artillery training centre by the Canadian Army. It was therefore thought that the Canadian soldier might have gone through that preliminary training centre, hence his mention of the University of Winnipeg and that he had been in the artillery. As such, the police reasoned that it did not of necessity follow that when he arrived in England that he would have been posted to an artillery unit.

The police also sent a letter to the Commissioner of the Canadian Military Police at Ottawa via the Canadian Military Police with the particulars of the man that they were looking for and asked for the records at Ottawa to be searched and enquiries made at Manitoba University with a view to establishing the Canadian soldiers' identity, but they didn't reply.

When the police made enquiries regarding the man being attached to the REME (the Royal Electrical and Mechanical Engineers) they found that the Canadian Army didn't have a unit bearing that name and that all personnel that were entitled to call themselves REME in the Canadian Army

were attached to the Royal Canadian
Ordnance Corps.

It was established that there were ten
divisions in the Canadian Army to which
men entitled to call themselves REME were
attached and they were in East Grinstead,
Godstone, Heathfield, Horsham,
Billinghurst, Cuckfield, Aldershot,
Farnborough, Cobham and Burgh Heath.
However, with the full assistance of the
commanding officers, over 1,000 such men
were interrogated and none of them were
considered to have been the man that they
were looking for. However, it was noted that
several men that were entitled to be called
REME had transferred to other units
although most of them were tracked down
by the police in their respective areas. As
such, the line of enquiry failed to reveal the
identity of the Canadian soldier.

At the inquest, Maurice Horner's wife said
that they both kept an open house for anyone
that wanted a meal or wanted to be put up
for the night. She added that Maurice Horner
often met people when travelling and asked
them home for a meal and said that they
kept extra food specially for that purpose.
She said that they also had an understanding
when they married that both his or her

friends or anyone wanting food or drink, could stay at their house.

The pathologist at the inquest stated that he found bruising around each of Maurice Horner's eyes as well as a number of puncture wounds about his body and at least nine lacerated wounds to his back, top and right side of his head. The pathologist noted that Maurice Horner's skull was thin, especially at the sides and spoke of his skull fractures. He also said that Maurice Horner had several bruises under the under surface of his brain. He concluded that Maurice Horner's cause of death was coma due to extra-dural haemorrhage, secondary to fractures of the skull. He also noted that he thought that Maurice Horner had been hit at least nine times, probably more, and that his injuries could not have been caused by merely falling or anything of that kind.

After the jury returned a verdict of murder by some person or persons unknown, the police noted that they had been greatly handicapped in the first instance because they were not informed of the matter until almost twelve hours after Maurice Horner was attacked. They noted that if they had been given the alarm at once, then it was more likely that the constable at the police box who spoke to the Canadian soldier at 12.45am might have made far more searching enquiries and might also have brought the soldier he spoke to to the police station.

However, it was also noted that they still had the clear single fingerprint that might still result in the crime being resolved as it was compared with all fingerprints of Canadian soldiers that were being arrested on an ongoing basis.

Marguerite Huber

Age: 18

Sex: female

Date: 3 Apr 1943

Place: 17 Manette Street, Westminster

Marguerite Huber died following an illegal operation with an instrument.

It was heard that there was no evidence connecting anyone with her death which was caused by a septic abortion and an open verdict was returned.

She was a cashier and had lived at 17 Manette Street in Westminster. She was taken to St Stephen's Hospital in Fulham on 25 March 1943 suffering from her injuries and later died on 3 April 1943.

Marguerite Huber's mother said that Marguerite Huber had been associating with a married cook who lived in Shaftesbury

Avenue with his wife and two children. She said that Marguerite Huber had been to an approved school for care and protection but ran away before she was 16 years old. She said that from what Marguerite Huber had told her that she would see the cook every day and that the cook would later go home to his wife each night.

Marguerite Huber's mother added that Marguerite Huber had told her who was responsible for her condition.

She said that she was first informed that Marguerite Huber had had a miscarriage when she got to the hospital and said that she knew of no one who might have interfered with her.

Marguerite Huber's mother said that on the morning of 24 March 1943 she met Marguerite Huber and that they later had some lunch together after then went to the pictures at Camden Town. She said that she later left Marguerite Huber at about 5.30pm at which time she seemed quite well, saying that Marguerite Huber told her that she had an appointment, but did not say where.

She said that Marguerite Huber never actually told her that she wished to end her pregnancy but said that Marguerite Huber 'knew that she must not have it'.

The doctor at St Stephen's Hospital said that when Marguerite Huber was admitted, she was suffering from a septic abortion and generalised peritonitis.

A doctor who had a surgery on Dean Street in Soho said that Marguerite Huber came to him on 25 January 1943 accompanied by the cook. He said that when he then examined Marguerite Huber he suspected that she was pregnant. He said that he first saw her on 24 September 1942 when he treated her for colitis and then again on 29 December 1942 when she complained of earache and toothache, and he gave her a prescription. The doctor said that when Marguerite Huber came to see him on 25 January 1943, Marguerite Huber asked him if it were possible to get rid of the baby, or words to that effect and said that he told her that it was not. The doctor added that neither Marguerite Huber or the cook asked him whether they knew of anyone who could get rid of the baby.

The doctor said that when Marguerite Huber next called for him to attend her at her home at 17 Monette Street on 25 Match 1943, he found that she was very ill and had signs of a threatened abortion and he made arrangements for her to be removed to hospital.

The pathologist that examined her said that her death was due to pelvic peritonitis consequent upon instrumental interference.

The cook said that he had known Marguerite Huber for about two years, but said that he did not know that she was going to have a baby. He said that when Marguerite Huber went to see the doctor it was because she had been feeling ill when she ate and denied that he had asked the doctor to examine Marguerite Huber to see whether she was pregnant.

He said that he had nothing to do with her death and didn't take her to anyone to have an illegal operation performed on her.

He said that he went with Marguerite Huber to see the doctor twice, the first time being in January 1943 when she had pains in her side and had been vomiting, noting that there was no thought that that time that she was going to have a baby. He said that he understood that the doctor had given Marguerite Huber some medicine in January

1943 which he said he understood was for gastritis. He said that in February and March 1943 Marguerite Huber's health was all right and that on the night of 24 March 1943 she was taken ill, but that she was all right again in the morning.

The cook said that later in the afternoon of 25 March 1943, he found her in bed shivering and said that he then asked for the doctor to call.

The doctor said that when he arrived at 17 Manette Street, he found Marguerite Huber suffering from the threatened abortion and noted that he was suspicious at that point that it might not have been a spontaneous abortion.

After the doctor gave his evidence at the inquest, the police stated that they didn't wish for an adjournment and an open verdict was returned.

Florence Mary Needham and Nicholas John Benjafield

Age: 59 and 3

Sex: female and male

Date: 21 Mar 1943

Place: Fulney Land Settlement, Spalding

Florence Mary Needham and her grandson Nicholas John Benjafield died at the same time at their home.

The coroners jury returned an open verdict in the case of Nicholas Benjafield, who died from nicotine poisoning, and stated that Florence Needham died from natural causes, shock, accelerated by cardiac weakness.

They were both found dead in the kitchen of their home, No. 17 Holding on the Fulney

Land Settlement in Spalding on the morning of 21 March 1943.

It was first thought that they had died from electrocution. However, after their organs were analysed, Nicholas Benjafield was found to have had a quantity of nicotine in his system but that Florence Needham had none.

It was noted that both Florence Needham and Nicholas Benjafield had both, a few minutes before their deaths, appeared quite well.

When the house was examined, no nicotine could be found or any vessel that might have contained it.

Nicholas Benjafield's 7-year-old sister said that when she got up, she went downstairs and saw 'nan-nan', Florence Needham, who gave her some porridge. She said that Florence Needham said that Nicholas Benjafield was to lie in bed a little time after which he could come down, which she said he did.

Nicholas Benjafield's 7-year-old sister said that she then went out to fetch the milk and that when she returned, whilst she could get in the outer door, she could not open the scullery door. She said that she then saw Nicholas Benjafield and Florence Needham on the floor.

The sister later said that she didn't think that Nicholas Benjafield had had anything to drink and also said that she didn't think that he had had any porridge as it was still in the pot.

The police said that when they questioned Nicholas Benjafield's 7-year-old sister, she told them that on the Saturday she had been playing with Nicholas Benjafield up the field and that they had found a bottle with some white stuff in it and that he had drunk out of it. She said that Nicholas Benjafield had found the bottle the previous week and had brought it back home but said that Nicholas Benjafield's 'daddy' had made him take it back.

Nicholas Benjafield's mother said that she last saw her mother, Florence Needham and her son alive at about midnight, noting that they were both alright at the time.

She said that the following morning she heard her daughter shouting from underneath her bedroom window, saying

that she could not get in and that she could
see Nicholas Benjafield in the kitchen asleep
on the floor without his shoes or socks on.
Nicholas Benjafield's mother said that she
then went downstairs and found Nicholas
Benjafield lying on the floor with his
serviette lying beneath him and Florence
Needham lying half against the copper, just
touching Nicholas Benjafield with a flue
brush in her hand.

At the inquest, Nicholas Benjafield's mother
said that she used to give Nicholas
Benjafield orange juice and cod-liver oil
every morning, but said that she didn't know
whether he had had any that morning. When
the orange juice bottle was examined, it was
empty.

A doctor that examined Nicholas Benjafield
said that Nicholas Benjafield had not been
sick and said that he would not expect him
to be from nicotine poisoning which he said
had a very quick action. He added that he
found no signs of violence and said that he
was certain that no outside person was
concerned with his death.

A doctor that carried out Florence
Needham's post-mortem said that she was
not by any means healthy. He said that she

had degeneration of the heart as well as long standing chronic bronchitis. He also said that she had a condition of the lower bowel that might have caused her death by obstruction in 12 months time. He added that there was no sign of violence having been used against her and nothing to show any poisoning. He said that her heart was in such a state that death might have been caused suddenly. He also said that there were no signs of electrocution and that an analysis of her stomach contents was negative. He concluded that Florence Needham died from natural causes through cardiac failure, adding that her death could undoubtedly have been caused by any shock or fright or by exertion, such as lifting Nicholas Benjafield when he was dead. He added that the case was just such a case where he might expect such a thing to happen.

When the doctor examined Nicholas Benjafield he said that he was a well-nourished and healthy child and that there was no natural cause of death. He said that an examination of his stomach revealed that he had recently had a meal and that there were signs of an irritant poisoning. He said that it appeared that his death had taken place very quickly and that he could find no outward trace of asphyxiation or electrocution.

The doctor said that nicotine was one of the most powerful poisons known to toxicologists and that death from it was very quick. He said that a few drops would kill and that a child was more susceptible than an adult. The doctor added that there were no signs of burning to Nicholas Benjafield's throat that might have indicated that he had been forced to take it and said that it had obviously been taken in a form that did not cause irritation to the mouth. The doctor added that having regard to what had been said of the form of nicotine found on such estates, that the poison was not taken in shreds. He said that two forms were possible, either liquid or crystals with the pure alkaloid itself. He noted that the third possibility of it being taken in capsule form was thought could be eliminated from the enquiry as no such capsules were found.

The doctor concluded that Nicholas Benjafield no doubt died from nicotine poisoning and that Florence Needham had died from natural causes accelerated by shock.

When the doctor was questioned, he said that he didn't think that the nicotine could have been taken the previous night and that he was certain that it took only a few minutes to kill Nicholas Benjafield.

A doctor from the Forensic Laboratory in Nottingham said that he found a number of grains of crude nicotine in Nicholas Benjafield's organs, which he said was enough to have killed several people. He further noted that there was no trace of nicotine in Florence Needham's system. The doctor said that if Nicholas Benjafield had taken the nicotine in capsule form then the capsule would have dissolved. He further stated that it was not possible to buy nicotine without signing the poison register. He also said that he had examined certain crockery, including the porridge pot, and found no traces of nicotine.

An estate manager with the Land Settlement Association in Low Fulney, said that nicotine was kept in flakes and liquid in locked cupboards in their stores and that no fumigating had been carried out at No. 17 holding in the previous 12 months. He said that only a sufficient quantity of nicotine was ever issued to tenants and that it was unlikely that there would have been any surplus quantity left about in the glasshouses. He said that very little nicotine was ever used and that in the previous twelve months only about four ounces had been issued. The man added that Nicholas Benjafield's father would not have required nicotine as he had no glasshouses on his premises.

It was further noted that only the storekeeper would have had access to the nicotine and that the keys for the store were kept at the office and handed out by the estate clerk.

A tomato grower employed by the estate that lived in Albert Street in Spalding said that the last issue of nicotine to him had been about twelve months ago and said that it had been in flake form. He said that he had taken the nicotine flakes to a glasshouse and then set fire to them and closed the door. He added that he had had no liquid form nicotine issued to him for the glasshouse in three years.

When an electricity engineer with the Spalding Urban Council made tests at the house with a view to determining the possibility of an electrocution, he said that the only place where an electrocution might have been caused was at a light switch. He said that he wetted his hands and touched the switch but said that there was no effect. He said that there was similarly no effect when he touched the water pipes. He said that he then made a thorough examination but could find no defects. He said that he then took the switch off and tested it, passing 16,5000 volts through it with no result and said that it took 19,5000 volts to break it down. He said that when he then replaced it in the scullery and passed 230 volts through it, it was perfectly clear. He said that when he inspected the wiring of the house, he found the workmanship was good and that the switches used were of good quality.

When the coroner summed up he said that he thought that they could rule out electrocution as the cause of death and suggested that Nicholas Benjafield had died from nicotine poisoning and that Florence Needham had died from natural causes, with the only question being as to how the nicotine got into the child.

The jury then, without retiring, returned an open verdict on Nicholas Benjafield and a verdict of death by natural causes on Florence Needham.

Mary Elizabeth Comins

Age: 33

Sex: female

Date: 21 Mar 1943

Place: Vine Street Bus Garage, Scarborough, Yorkshire

Mary Elizabeth Comins was killed in a disused bus garage at Scarborough, Yorkshire, on 21 March 1943.

Her body was found in a few inches of water in an inspection pit in the garage by a little girl that had been playing in the garage on the night of Wednesday 24 March 1943.

Her injuries were described as minimal, but she was found to have been strangled.

She was last seen on the Sunday 21 March 1943 at about 11pm and it was thought that she had died within a few hours after her last sighting. Her body was not found until three days later.

The bus garage had been occupied by military authorities up to a few hours of the murder.

She had been wearing a black lambswool coat and a small grey felt hat and was fully dressed when found. There were no signs of a struggle and it was thought that she had gone into the garage voluntarily.

She had been out the previous evening with a friend and two soldiers and was last seen later that night with a soldier who was not traced, and it was thought certain that the soldier she had been with had gone off with her and killed her.

It was reported that the police were investigating a tangled 'Number 7' clue that they found in the bus garage. It was said that the 'No. 7' had a forces origin.

The police said that they had extended their search to Richmond, the Midlands and Wiltshire. It was thought that Mary Comins might have had a secret friendship with a temporary visitor to the town and police sought to examine all late-night passes and weekend passes that were issued between 20 March and 22 March 1943.

She had lived in Wrea Lane in Scarborough and her husband had been serving in the Middle East at the time.

Her father, who lived alone in Vine Street, Middlesbrough, was an old man and it was reported that, so he could spend his last days with peace of mind, he was not told about Mary Comins's murder. One of his sons said, 'We are determined to keep the news of Mary's death from father. He has had a stroke and is dangerously ill, and we fear that the shock of hearing of her death might kill him'.

Mary Comins had worked as an assistant at a grocer's shop.

Baby

Age: 0

Sex: male

Date: 20 Mar 1943

Place: Newhall

The body of a newly-born child was found in a garage in Newhall on Saturday 20 March 1943.

The medical evidence showed that the child had knife wounds on its skull, throat and shoulder and that the child had been born normally.

The coroner returned a verdict of murder by some person or persons unknown.

Maureen Ritchie

Age: 22 months

Sex: female

Date: 28 Feb 1943

Place: Broxton Manor, Four Elms

Maureen Ritchie died from a fractured skull.

She had lived at 17 Market Field Road in Redhill with her mother but her mother had taken her to Broxton Hall in Four Elms in September 1942 after seeing an advert in a paper for a home for children whose mothers were on war work or could not devote their full time to them.

When Maureen Ritchie's mother took her there she had been fit and well, but her mother received a telegram on 1 March 1943 as well as a telephone message asking her to come to the home at once and when she did she found that Maureen Ritchie was dead.

She had died from a fractured skull and an open verdict was returned.

The woman that ran Broxton Hall said that she had rented it since 1942 and that she was not a qualified nurse. She said that she inserted an advertisement in the newspaper and that as a result Maureen Ritchie was brought to the home. She said that Maureen Ritchie had one or two fits during her stay as well as another one on 28 February 1943 and said that she then sent for a doctor but by the time he arrived she was dead.

She added that she had never hit Maureen Ritchie on the head.

The doctor said that he saw Maureen Ritchie some time before Christmas and said that her health at that time was good. He said that he sent her to Tunbridge Wells for an X-Ray as she had something the matter with her arm and said that it was later found that she had a fractured skull as well as a new and an old fracture of the arm. He said that he didn't see her again until after her death.

The radiologist at the Kent and Sussex Hospital said that Maureen Ritchie had had a fractured skull and arm but said that he could not say how recent they were.

The pathologist carried out a post-mortem on 2 March 1943 and said that he found numerous bruises on Maureen Ritchie's body, a fractured skull, and a fracture of both bones of her forearm.

However, the coroner's jury said that there was insufficient evidence to show how the fracture to her skull was caused and an open verdict was returned.

John Neill

Age: 54

Sex: male

Date: 25 Feb 1943

Place: Stanley Warehouse, Regent Road, Liverpool

John Neill was shot at about 10.25pm on Thursday 25 February 1943 on the 9th floor of Stanley Warehouse on Regent Road in Liverpool.

He was shot by an American soldier that was on guard duty at the warehouse where he was working.

The case was put forward by the Director of Public Prosecutions, but was not brought to trial.

The greater part of Stanley Warehouse in Regent Road Liverpool was used as a store by the United States Army and a large number of dock labourers were employed there trucking and stacking the goods.

The 9th floor was divided by four consecutive sections, A, B, C and D respectively and each section was divided from the next by two sets of double doors that were left open in the sections where the dock labourers were working.

On the night of 25 February 1943 20 dock labourers were working on the 9th floor, 10 in C Section and 10 in D Section. There was also a large goods and passenger lift working in B Section and consequently the doors dividing B Section and C Section were not closed although the dock labourers were not working on the floor of B Section even though they were using the lift there. The doors between A Section and B Section were as such closed.

There was an armed sentry patrolling each floor whilst work was in progress and his duty was to protect the Army Stores against pilferage or wilful damage.

John Neill, who lived at 8 House, 6 Court, Upper William Street in Liverpool was a dock labourer and had been in charge of the gang working in D Section.

The soldier that shot him was 29-years old and was a 1st Class Private in the 156th

Infantry Detachment, APO 507 US Army and had been on sentry duty on the 9th floor of the warehouse and had been armed with a rifle that was loaded with 8 rounds of ammunition.

It was found that shortly before 10pm on 25 February 1943 the dock labourers in D Section had been trucking cardboard cartons of Army boots and the soldier had taken exception to the rough manner in which they were handling the goods and he spoke to John Neill about it. However, an argument developed that was thought to have gone on for some time, first in D Section and then in C Section. However, the man in charge of C Section said that he could see that the argument was going to lead to serious trouble and he said that he stepped in between the two men and took John Neill back to his section and the soldier went off in the opposite direction towards B Section.

However, a few minutes later the man in charge of C Section said that he saw John Neill walking towards B Section, but thought that he was just going down the lift to have a smoke, and as he wanted to have a smoke too, he went to do the same and followed John Neill towards B Section. However, he said that John Neill went past the lift to the far end of B Section and that a few moments later he saw a flash and heard the report of a gun and then saw John Neill fall by some packages. He said that he didn't see who fired the shot but said that as he approached John Neill to help him, he saw the soldier who told him to get back and so he went back to his own section.

Another dock labourer who lived at 3 Bickerton Street in Liverpool and who was a floorman on the 9th floor said that at about 10.45pm on the Thursday 25 February 1943 he had been walking along B Section gangway towards A Section when he saw John Neill walking in front of him in the same direction and said that in front of John Neill he saw the soldier. He said that there was about 10 yards between them and that he then saw a flash and heard a shot, noting that the flash came from the soldier. He said that he then saw John Neill spin around and fall behind some cases.

The dock labourer said that he continued to walk in the same direction towards A Section when the soldier, who he said was standing practically up against the iron doors between A Section and B Section said to him, 'Get back' or 'Stand back'. The dock labourer said that he then said, 'You've shot the man', and said that the soldier then repeated, 'Get back' or 'Stand back'. The dock labourer said that he then went back to C Section where he made a telephone call to tell someone what had happened.

Three other dock labourers also made statements detailing the argument between John Neill and the soldier, but they didn't see the shooting.

A staff sergeant who had been in the office on the ground floor of the warehouse said that he got a telephone call at about 10.25pm and as a consequence, he went up to the 9th floor of the warehouse with a lieutenant and some other officers where he saw John Neill and the soldier in the doorway between B Section and C Section, noting that his rifle was in the post-arms position and that there was a crowd of men standing about 12 yards from him. He said that when he asked the soldier what had happened the soldier said, 'We got in an argument and I shot a man' and turned around and pointed along the gangway. The staff sergeant said that he then went in the direction that the soldier indicated along the gangway and saw John Neill on the floor with a wound in his back, apparently dead.

When the lieutenant asked the soldier again what had happened, he said, 'The men were handling the cases roughly and I told them to be more careful. The crew leader agreed with me and told the men to be careful. A few minutes later I noticed that the men were handling the cases rough and I told them again. The crew leader didn't like it and said it was none of my business how they handle them. I told them that it was my orders and could prove it by the Sergeant of the Guard. I started to the telephone to call the Sergeant and the crew started ganging round me. I stepped back and the crew leader started calling me names. I walked away to keep from having any trouble. The crew leader followed me, still cursing. I walked as far back as I could. The crew leader wanted to fight. I threw my gun on him and told him not to come any closer. He kept walking in at the gun and I shot him'.

The soldier was then disarmed and placed under arrest and later detained at Seaforth Barracks.

When the police arrived and examined the scene they said that it appeared that after being struck by the bullet, John Neill appeared to have staggered about a yard from the middle of the main gangway and then twisted round and to have fallen against a tier of packages which were found to have been heavily bloodstained. He was found lying face downwards and inclined to his right-hand side with his arms outstretched. The police noted that his overcoat was almost removed from his body and that all but the right sleeve just above the elbow was off and that there appeared to be little doubt that John Neill had been in the act of removing his overcoat when he was shot and that as such, there was reason to believe that he had been about to attack the soldier.

After a lengthy search, the bullet was discovered to have passed through John Neill's body and to have struck a concrete pillar that had caused it to break into small pieces. One or two pieces were recovered from the floor and the other pieces were recovered from inside a carton of boots.

When the soldier's rifle was taken and examined, it was found to contain 7 live rounds of ammunition and one empty cartridge case.

During the medical examination of John Neill, liquid was found flowing from his mouth and there was found to be a strong smell of alcohol.

When the police questioned the soldier, he said, 'I have nothing to say to the civil authorities about it'. When he was told that he might be charged with wilful murder he made no reply.

The case was brought to the Director of Public Prosecutions for consideration, but no charges were made.

William Olding

Age: 48

Sex: male

Date: 21 Feb 1943

Place: Feltham

William Olding was knocked over on the road by a lorry on 16 February 1943 and later died in hospital on 21 February 1943.

An open verdict was returned at his inquest after it was heard that it was not possible to state definitely which lorry in a convoy of lorries passing over the railway bridge at Feltham on 16 February 1943 had been responsible for colliding with him.

William Olding's wife said that William Olding was a healthy man and had been cycling to and from work for years and was not subject to giddy or fainting attacks.

The doctor that carried out William Olding's post-mortem said that William Olding's death was due to hypostatic pneumonia, laceration of the left lung, and fractures to the whole of his rib ribs and scapula. He added that there was nothing to indicate that William Olding had lost consciousness prior to being knocked down.

A man that lived on Lansbury Avenue in Feltham said that he was cycling behind William Olding up Feltham Bridge who he said was about a foot from the curb. He said that an Army troop-carrying lorry then overtook him and swerved out to pass another cyclist ahead of him who chad been riding about 5feet from the kerb. He said that the lorry then straightened up and that he then noticed that the back of the lorry appeared to be swinging. He said that his view of William Olding was obscured, and that the next thing that he saw was someone appearing at the back of the lorry and fall. He said that he didn't see any impact.

The cyclist said that he thought that the lorry was going to stop but said that it didn't but noted that he thought that the soldiers in it must have seen him waving and pointing to the roadway and must have seen William Olding lying there.

The man said that he then took steps to establish who had been in the lorry and then went to William Olding's assistance.

When asked what steps he took to find out who had been driving the lorry, the man said that he stopped the next lorry and asked them who had been driving the lorry in front of him, but said that the lorry driver had told him that he didn't know.

The cyclist that had been in front of the other man and behind William Olding said that he had been endeavouring to catch up with William Olding who he said was about a dozen paces in front of him. He said that the troop carrier passed him with about three feet clearance, but then cut in front of William Olding. He said that he then saw a portion of the nearside body of the carrier then strike William Olding, at which point he said that the bonnet of the carrier had passed William Olding. He added that he could not understand why the driver had cut in as he had done as there had been nothing coming from the opposite direction. He said that after William Olding was knocked over, both he and the other cyclist shouted for the lorry to stop but said that it didn't. He also said that he thought that the troops in the lorry must have seen William Olding lying in the road.

A civilian lorry driver who lived in Martindale Road, Hounslow said that he was detailed to take a convoy of troops and had been driving the fourth carrier in a convoy of eight. He said that as he approached the bridge, he saw a crowd on it and was stopped by a man who told him that the lorry in front of him had been involved in a collision. However, he said that he could not recall who had been driving the lorry that was in front of him. He said that the lorry in front of him had been about 200 to 300 yards ahead due to him being held up in Feltham High Street.

However, he said that when he arrived at Hounslow he spoke to the other drivers and a private said that he had been driving the preceding lorry but said that he didn't recall anything of the incident. The driver of the third lorry said that he did not recall passing any cyclist on Feltham Bridge and felt nothing of an accident. He said that the first that he heard of it was when another man asked him whether he knew anything of a mishap, by which time he had discharged his load of troops. He added that no one on the lorry had called his attention to an accident and said that in fact he had had an uneventful journey with traffic being dense in Feltham.

A policeman who took particulars after the accident said that there was no damage to William Olding's bicycle beyond a slight twist in the steering head.

Another policeman that went to examine the first five lorries of the convoy said that he could find no marks on any of them to suggest an impact.

When the coroner summed up, he said that the question of the identity of the lorry caused him some difficulty as there was no definite evidence as to which one was involved. He noted that no one took the number of the lorry and that it was only a process of deduction that had narrowed down the lorry to the one driven by the private. He also added that if it was the front part of the body of the lorry that had struck William Olding then it would have been outside the vision of the driver.

As such, the coroner said that in his view the evidence was insufficient to justify fastening the accident on to the lorry driven by the private and that in the absence of definite proof that the private had been driving the lorry that struck William Olding, or that the order of the procession of lorries was not altered on the journey, he would return an open verdict stating that there was insufficient evidence to determine how William Olding's injuries were caused.

John Henry Hillman

Age: 69

Sex: male

Date: 13 Feb 1943

Place: Bleadon Hill, Somerset

John Henry Hillman was found dead in some gorse bushes on Bleadon Hill.

His body was found by a man that had been out rabbiting.

He had lived at 12 Meadow Villas in Weston-super-Mare.

He was found on the Saturday 13 February 1943 after having gone missing in October 1942.

His wife said that he had left home on 12 October 1942 saying that if he was not back for lunch that he would be back at about 2pm but said that she never saw him alive again. She said that she first thought that he had gone to see relatives in Trowbridge, but when he didn't return, she called the police.

She said that John Hillman had suffered from heart trouble and said that part of their home was destroyed in the blitz.

The medical evidence stated that when found, his body was for the most part a skeleton. A pathologist said that he could find no evidence of poison or violence.

His inquest returned an open verdict stating that he was found dead on Bleadon Hill, but that there was nothing to indicate how he had died. The coroner added that it was possible that John Hillman had climbed the hill and after feeling symptoms of heart trouble had laid down.

John Hillman had formerly been a coal merchant as well as a councillor in Weston-super-Mare.

Joseph Powell

Age: unknown

Sex: male

Date: 13 Feb 1943

Place: Ivy House, Copse Cross Street, Ross-on-Wye, Herefordshire

Joseph Powell was shot in the head in his billet in Ross-on-Wye, Herefordshire.

A 23-year-old soldier was tried for his murder at the Old Bailey but was acquitted.

Joseph Powell was a Lance Corporal.

The soldier said that he had never had any kind of quarrel with Joseph Powell and that they had been in the same platoon since 1940. He said that as he was entering Ivy House he heard a shot fired and denied that he had had taken or loaded the rifle or that he had fired the shot that killed Joseph Powell.

The medical evidence stated that the bullet entered Joseph Powell's mouth and came out of the back of his head where it made a hole in the wall. It was said that the shot had been fired from about the doorway of his room from the shoulder of an averaged height man.

Joseph Powell had been on the top bunk in his room when he was shot. The bullet made a hole in the plaster of the wall just above the head of the bed between the greatcoat and the service respirator that was hanging on the wall.

The soldier that was tried for his murder had been playing cards with some other men during the afternoon and after tea, that evening he visited several public houses between 7.20pm and 10pm and visited the Harp public house which was about three minutes walking distance from Ivy House.

When the pub shut the soldier was seen by others, but he did not walk back with them and when the other soldiers got back they found that the soldier had got back before them and that he was in his room. They said that when they got back the soldier went into another room and sat by the fire for some time and appeared to be in a moody state of mind.

At about 10.15pm, two soldiers went into the room and found Joseph Powell preparing to get into bed. However, they only remained for a matter of minutes in his room before leaving him alone.

It was said however that the soldier then left the room at about 10.25pm and didn't return again until sometime after the firing of the shot five minutes later at about 10.30pm.

The soldier was arrested soon after at 1.20am in the early hours of 14 February 1943.

In his statement he said that he went in at 10.30pm and he heard a shot at the door of his room which was on the ground floor and then met two other soldiers who also heard the shot and said that he said, 'I will go upstairs with you and see what it is'. He said that one of the other soldiers led the way and when they went into the room that Joseph Powell slept in he was dead on his bed. He said that they then went downstairs and woke up the Lance Corporal and told him what was up and said that the Lance Corporal then went up to see Joseph Powell and tested his heart and then said, 'He is dead'. He said that the Lance Corporal then told everyone to get out of the room and then stood guard at the door and an officer was sent for. He said that when a Captain who was in charge of an anti-tank platoon came, he inspected all the rifles in the room that Joseph Powell was in.

In a further statement he added that he had been in the Lance Corporals room at about 10.05pm after which he went to his own room where he changed his shoes, putting on his sand-shoes, and that he then went to the urinal and then came back and then met the other two soldiers and heard the shot.

In a later statement that he made on 15 February 1943, he said, 'I was in my billet at Ivy House in the Lance Corporals room, that is the first room on the left going in. We were playing cards, three card brag. The Lance corporal was there, but not Joseph Powell. There were others I did not know. After finishing playing cards at about five minutes to five I went to my own room, the second room on the right opposite the wash-place to get my pot and went to the barrel yard for tea. After tea I returned to my billet at about 6 o'clock. This was on Saturday 13th February 1943. I then had a shave in my own room. Another private was there. The other private went out before me and I then went to the Lance Corporal's room but did not play cards. I remained there about ten minutes and I then went out on my own and stood on the pavement opposite the George Hotel until about 7.10pm. I then went to the Harp Inn and had a drink. I had about five pints and one bottle of stout. When I visited the Harp Inn it was 7.20pm. I remained there until one minute to ten when I left. Earlier in the evening the private and another private came to the Harp. After leaving the Harp I went direct to my billet arriving there at about five past ten pm. Upon entering my room, I changed my shoes and put on sand shoes. I remained in my billet all that afternoon on 13th February 1943 playing cards as I have stated'.

The soldier denied shooting Joseph Powell and said that it might have been someone indulging in horseplay or fooling and that they might have fired the shot meaning to give Joseph Powell a fright and that they had instead shot him.

A private that had been billeted at Ivy House in room 2 said that Joseph Powell and another man had been sleeping in room 4.

He said that on 13 February 1943 that he
went to tea at the Barrell Inn Yard and that
in the afternoon he played cards in his room
with a number of other soldiers including
the soldier tried for the murder. He said that
after tea he returned to his billet at about
5.30pm after which he went out to the
cinema. He said that after that, between
10.05pm and 10.10pm he went straight back
to his billet and went to his room. He said
that there were a number of other men there
including the Lance Corporal, two other
privates and the soldier tried for murder. He
said that the wireless was on and that the
soldier was sitting on a box near the fire
wearing his khaki trousers, gym shoes and a
khaki pullover. He said that he said to him,
'You've had a good day, haven't you?',
meaning that he had won something at cards
and said that the soldier replied 'Yes'.
However, he said that he seemed very
moody and that he had one hand in his
mouth and was looking into the fireplace
and was slobbering.

The private said that when he turned to
speak to the Lance Corporal, the soldier
went out of the room and that he then got
into bed. He said that shortly after 10.30pm
he heard an announcement on the wireless,
'Music while you work' and that while the

programme was being announced he heard a shot. He said that the door to his room was closed and that shortly after one of the other privates who slept in the room on the opposite side of the passage, room 2, opened it and came in followed by another private. He said that the shot appeared to have been fired from up above him, upstairs, and that one of the privates then woke the Lance Corporal up and they then both went upstairs. He said that he then put on his trousers and went out into the passage and then upstairs with the other private and the Lance Corporal, immediately in front of them. He said that while they were going upstairs the other private and the Lance Corporal then passed him and went into room 4 where Joseph Powell slept. He said that the light was on and that when he looked in he saw Joseph Powell lying on the top bunk in the opposite corner from the door. He said that there was a very strong smell of cordite and that they all went into the room together and that the Lance Corporal looked at Joseph Powell.

The private said that he did not see the other soldier from the time that he had left his room earlier until he was in room 4 where Joseph Powell was lying dead in his bunk, and said that whilst they were there the soldier came along with a number of other soldiers.

The Captain who arrived after being called was with the Royal Army Medical Corp attached to the Kings Own Yorkshire Infantry stationed in Ross. He said that when he went into room 4 he saw the body of Joseph Powell on the top bunk of a double tier opposite the door in the corner. He said that there was a quantity of blood on the upper and lower bunks and that on examination he found that there was a bullet wound through Joseph Powell's lower lip that passed through the hard palate and that there was an exit wound at the back of his skull from which there was an extrusion of brain matter. He added that there was also a grooved bullet wound to the inner border of Joseph Powell's right hand. He said that then, in the wall behind the bed there was a hole around which there were pieces of brain tissue. He said that in his opinion death had been instantaneous and that his wound was consistent with having been caused by a bullet from a service rifle.

The Captain said that he examined one rifle that had been brought into the room and said that the barrel of it looked as though it had been fired recently.

He said that he attended the post-mortem the following day which concluded that the shot was consistent with having been fired from a distance of several feet away. He said that the line of projection or the route of the bullet, indicated that it had been fired from about shoulder level of a man about 5ft 6in tall who had been standing in the doorway to the room.

A private in the Kings Own Yorkshire Light Infantry stationed at Ross said that he had been sleeping in room 5 and that he had gone to his room to go to bed at approximately 10.30pm and turned out his light, noting that the two other soldiers in the room had already gone to bed. He said that shortly after he got into bed, he was disturbed by a man who came into the room. He said that he sat up and shouted, 'Who's there' and said that the man said, 'Keep quiet'. He said that the man came towards the bed and struck a petrol lighter and that by the light of it he saw that it was the soldier that was tried for the murder. He said that the soldier then blew out the lighter and then went to the window and seemed to grab a rifle that had been standing in the corner by the window, noting that he thought that because he heard the bump of a butt on the floor. He said that the man then went to the mantlepiece and then towards the door and said that he then heard a noise like a rifle being loaded just before he went, noting that it was the click of a bolt. He said that he then heard the man run down the passage and immediately after heard a rifle shot. He said that by the sound of the soldiers footsteps in the room he seemed to have been wearing gym shoes.

The private said that after the shot the man seemed to come running back and said that he heard a noise as if he was putting the rifle back in the corner of the bedroom, on the right hand side of the door just inside and that after replacing the rifle he heard the soldier run back off down the passage.

The private said that he then put on the light and partially dressed and saw three rifles in the corner to the right of the door. He said that there had been two live .303 rounds on the mantlepiece at about 6pm, noting that they had been there for about two months, and said that when he then looked there in the morning there was only one.

One of the other soldiers that had been in room 5 said that he heard a person come in shortly after the other private had gone to bed, saying that he heard him speak, and said that when the person left he heard the sound of a rifle bolt and soon after a shot. He said that he then heard the door open and the sound of a rifle being put against the wall on the right-hand side of the doorway and said that he then got up and dressed and went out into the passage and then went back to bed. He said that he had been in bed for about ten minutes when the soldier came into the room, noting that the light was on at that time, having been switched on by someone after he had heard the shot, and said that he saw the soldier take a towel out of the front of his trousers and after looking about the room bend down and cleaned the outside of one of the three rifles with it. He said that he saw him clean round the trigger guard and bolt and said that when he asked him what he was doing the soldier replied, 'Keep quiet, you know nothing', and then he left the room.

After finding Joseph Powell, a Captain with the Kings Own Yorkshire Light Infantry said that he went into room 5 and inspected the three rifles there and took one of them that he thought had been fired recently. He said that he noticed that the action was cocked, and that the safety catch applied as soon as it was picked up. He said that none of the other rifles there had been fired.

When the rifle was examined by an Armourer with the Royal Electrical and Mechanical Engineers attached to the Kings Own Yorkshire Light Infantry stationed at Ross, he said that he formed the opinion that it had recently been fired. He said that the barrel was foul by the gases from a discharged round and that he was of the opinion that it had been fired within six hours because it had not yet started to properly sweat. He said that the following morning he examined twenty-eight other rifles and said that none of them had been fired for several days.

Following the initial enquiries, the soldier was charged with the murder of Joseph Powell at 4am on 14 February 1943 but was later acquitted at his trial.

Gladys Merrick

Age: 16

Sex: female

Date: 8 Feb 1943

Place: Reform Club, Goldthorpe

Gladys Merrick was found strangled on a piece of waste ground on Monday 8 February 1943 at about 11.15am by a pensioner who was taking his usual morning walk along the path at the back of the Reform Club in Goldthorpe.

She was found semi-nude with her clothing was torn and she had marks on her throat. She was said to have still had on her socks and shoes. The land she was found on was described as a piece of waste land which was behind the Reform Club in Goldthorpe by the common.

She was a munition girl and had lived at 38 Briton Street in Thurnscoe.

She was about 5ft 3in tall with fair hair and grey-blue eyes.

She had left home the previous evening, Sunday 7 February 1943, at about 7.15pm, wearing a blue blouse and skirt, a three-quarter length brown coat, blue overalls, a brown scarf with yellow stripes, and a yellow scarf which she had worn as a turban. When she was found her clothing was found strewn about her.

It wasn't until later on the Monday that she was identified. Her mother found out after hearing some women talking about the murder in a queue, and when she asked who the girl was, she found out that it was her daughter.

The Reform Club was just off the main road and Gladys Merrick was found lying about 15 yards from the road.

The doorkeeper at the club said that he had not seen Gladys Merrick enter the club on the Sunday and said that only one woman, who had been wearing trousers, had entered.

The Club Steward whose bedroom window was about ten yards from where Gladys Merrick's body was found said that he had been up until late on the Sunday night but heard nothing fom outside.

Another woman that lived nearby said that heard the sound of a person running and a scream, and another woman who lived in a bungalow next to the plot of land where Gladys Merrick was found said that she thought that she heard a scream at about 9.15pm on the Sunday.

However, it was also heard that it was not uncommon to hear screams and the shouts of girls at about that time.

Her mother said that when Gladys Merrick went out she promised to be back by 9.30pm which was the time that she was specified to be back by. However, when she failed to return, her mother said that she was not too concerned and made no enquiries as she knew that Gladys Merrick was in the habit of visiting her grandfather who lived at the other end of Goldthorpe.

She said that Gladys Merrick used to go out and stand by the doorways to the local dance halls and watch the dancers.

A neighbour said that Gladys Merrick came into her house just before 7pm on the

Sunday 7 February 1943 to see her husband to ask him to cut out some soles for her shoes, saying that she had 'somebody to see'.

It was not known what she had done between leaving her home and being murdered.

Thomas Hayes

Age: 22

Sex: male

Date: 29 Jan 1943

Place: Runcorn, Cheshire

Thomas Hayes was found with injuries in a field and was taken to Runcorn Cottage Hospital where he later died.

He was a farm labourer and had lived in Halton Road, Runcorn.

He had worked at Halton Gate Farm since he was a boy and on the Wednesday he and another farm worker had been carting turnips from Norton Priory which was about half a mile away from Halton Gate Farm.

The cart was pulled by two horses, one of which had been bought the day before, however, the employer said that he was satisfied that it was a quiet animal.

Thomas Hayes had made the first journey with the other farm worker, but when he prepared for the second trip he said that he could manage alone.

Later on the other farm worker and the employer had been loading straw in the farmyard when a horse that was attached to the cart came trotting back into the yard.

When they then went to investigate, they found Thomas Hayes in a field about a quarter of a mile away and the other horse roaming about in a turnip field with its chains still fastened to its collar.

When they went up to Thomas Hayes they found him lying unconscious in a pool of blood.

A doctor that examined his body said that his death was due to a fracture to the base of his skull. He said that he didn't think that his injuries were caused by him having been run over by his cart or by a horse hitting him in the head with its hooves, stating that the injuries to his scalp didn't indicate the outline of a horse's hoof.

The coroner said that he was satisfied that Thomas Hayes's employer had taken all reasonable precautions and stated that the medical evidence had not allowed him to form any opinion as to how his injuries had been caused.

Charles Gallagher

Age: 70

Sex: male

Date: 27 Jan 1943

Place: Harelawside, Grantshouse, Berwickshire

Charles Gallagher died after running out onto a road.

A lorry driver that passed him on 26 January 1943 said that he saw Charles Gallagher stagger out into the road in front of his lorry and said that when he pulled over and went back to see him, he found him lying in the road. Charles Gallagher was taken to Berwick Infirmary where he died from a skull injury the following day, 27 January 1943 at 5am.

It was found that there were no marks on the lorry and the coroner said that what troubled him was that it was not possible to say how his injuries had been caused and an open verdict was returned.

The doctor that treated Charles Gallagher said that when Charles Gallagher was brought into the infirmary at 10pm on 26 January 1943 he was deeply unconscious and had a small wound to the back of his head which had cut down to the bone.

When the doctor carried out the post-mortem, he said that he found that the brain substance on the left side of his head had been ploughed up. He added that there was no fracture to his skull and that his heart and other organs were quite normal for his age.

He said that he thought that his head injury was due to him falling on the back of his head.

A man from Howpark Farm in Granthouse who knew by sight said that on the night of 26 January 1943 he had passed Charles Gallagher on the road at about 8pm, going in the opposite direction, and that he had been walking in the middle of the road. He said that it was dark at the time and that he formed the opinion that Charles Gallagher had been under the influence of intoxicating liquor.

A rabbit trapper who lived at Harelawside Farm said that he was in his house near the road when the lorry driver came to the door of his house at about 8.10pm and asked for a light as he had knocked somebody down. He said that he got a torch and then went back with the driver to see. He said that the night was dark but that the road was dry and that when he went out with the lorry driver, he saw a big lorry standing on the road facing towards Berwick which had lights showing to its front.

He said that just in front of the offside driving wheel he then saw Charles Gallagher lying on the road on his back at an angle with his head pointing in the Grantshouse direction. He said that he was just over the white line in the centre of the road and that the lorry was standing on its nearside.

He said that he recognised the man as Charles Gallagher and that he then sent his wife off for coats and rugs to cover Charles Gallagher who was still alive and then telephoned for the police.

He said that when he called the police they told him to take Charles Gallagher into his house which he then did.

An ambulance then later arrived and took Charles Gallagher to the Berwick Infirmary.

When the rabbit trapper was questioned, he said that it would have been possible to have walked on the grass verge but that it would have been very rough going.

A policeman that arrived soon after said that when he arrived, he saw the lorry, which he said was about 50 feet in length, standing on the road facing Berwick with its near-side front-wheels about two and a half feet on the grass verge. He said that he also found some heavy tyre marks on the road that appeared to have been caused by the heavy application of brakes. He said that the marks extended for 78 feet from the driving wheel of the lorry. He said that the road surface was dry and that the road at the locus was practically straight for 100 yards west and 200 yards east. He added that the lorry had been showing four side lights to the front and a red light to the rear.

The policeman said that when he questioned the lorry driver, he told him that he had been going towards Berwick, travelling at a moderate speed and that after rounding a slight turn in the roadway he saw Charles Gallagher walking towards his vehicle. He said that he was walking on his nearside of the road and that that he saw nothing unusual in his conduct and continued to drive along the road. However, he said that as he drew very close to Charles Gallagher, he took a staggering run across the road in the direction of his lorry. He said that he then immediately applied his brakes and pulled the front portion of his lorry on to the grass verge of his nearside.

However, he added that at the time he was not aware that an accident had happened as he had felt no bump and said that the reason he stopped and got out of his cab was to give Charles Gallagher a good 'talking to'.

He said that when he walked to the rear of his lorry, he didn't see anything, but that when he returned his foot touched something and that when he looked, he saw that it was Charles Gallagher lying on the road.

When the coroner summed up he noted that although the incident happened over the Border of Scotland, it fell to him to conduct the inquiry by reason of the fact that Charles Gallagher had died in the Berwick Infirmary. He added that he was quite satisfied in his own mind that the driver of the lorry was in no way to blame for what had happened.

He noted that it did appear that Charles Gallagher had been drinking on the night but said that he was unable to state how his head injury occurred and returned an open verdict, stating that Charles Gallagher had died from cerebral haemorrhage following an injury to the skull, but that there was not sufficient evidence to show how that injury was received.

Charles Gallagher lived at Harelawside Farm.

William Pearce

Age: 59

Sex: male

Date: 20 Jan 1943

Place: Queens Bridge, Lacock

William Pearce was found lying in the road with injuries near the Queen's Bridge in Lacock.

He had gone out for a walk on the morning of 13 January 1943 and was found on the road at about 11am and was taken to the hospital and died on 20 January 1943.

He was an inmate of the Chippenham Public Assistance Institution.

The distance from the bridge to the road was 35 feet, and it was thought that from his injuries and his position that he might have fallen from the bridge, however, when he was found he denied having been on the bridge.

He had been admitted to the Chippenham Public Assistance Institution on 20 July 1942 having previously been at the Stratton Institution.

His health was described as being fairly good, but he was said to have imagined that he had stomach trouble.

It was heard that he appeared quite normal on the morning he went out for his usual walk on 13 January 1943 and it was noted that he was more often out than in and that he would just come in for meals.

After he was found he was taken to the Chippenham and District Hospital in an ambulance but arranged to be brought back to the Institution.

He was described as being in a very shocked condition and didn't seem to know what had happened and denied having been on the railway line. When he later recovered, he was asked again about having been on the railway line and was said to have appeared surprised that he should be asked, and repeated that he remembered nothing other than that he went out for a stroll.

A doctor that treated him observed that William Pearce did not appear to be the sort of person who might wish to take their own life.

The doctor that examined William Pearce when he arrived at the hospital said that he had a compound fracture of the right elbow, a fractured right femur, a fractured pelvis and other injuries, and added that he was in a very shocked condition. However, he said that after some blood transfusions and shock treatment his condition improved sufficiently to allow him to be transferred to Stratton St Margaret Hospital for surgical treatment which he said was urgently necessary. However, William Pearce later died there on 20 January 1943.

The doctor noted that William Pearce had imagined that he had been suffering from gastric trouble but said that he could never discover anything the matter with him. He added that William Pearce had been rather depressed at one time but said that there was nothing mentally wrong with him.

He said that there were no indications that William Pearce had been run over, but also noted that it was possible that he had been knocked down but concluded that his injuries were consistent with him having fallen from the bridge.

A lad that lived at Showell Cottages said that at about 9.30am on 13 January 1943 he was standing at the road junction with his back to Queen's Bridge when he heard a bang and then somebody groaning. He said that when he then went through the bridge, he saw William Pearce lying on the road. He noted that he saw no traffic passing at the time.

Another person that lived in Queen's Bridge said that he had met William Pearce at about 9.30am on the morning of 13 January 1943 at which time William Pearce had been walking away from the bridge.

A woman that lived at Patterdown House came out after the alarm was raised and brought rugs out to cover William Pearce while they waited for the ambulance. She said that as they waited, she asked William Pearce what had happened and said that he replied, 'No, I think I must have fallen or was hit'. She said that she also asked him whether he had been on the railway line but said that he replied, 'No, I have done nothing'.

A man that examined the place where William Pearce was found said that he had been found directly under the parapet of the bridge and noted that there were no marks on the road or the bridge.

When the coroner summed up he said that it was a rather peculiar case, stating that there seemed to be no sign of any vehicle that might have knocked William Pearce down and no reason for him to have thrown himself over the top of the parapet, and an open verdict was returned stating that William Pearce died from injuries from which he had been suffering when he was found on the highway.

Jan Von Der Spek

Age: 59

Sex: male

Date: 11 Jan 1943

Place: Liverpool

Jan Von Der Spek was found dead in a disused basement at Messrs. Lewis's Stores in Liverpool on Monday 11 January 1943.

He was found with a fractured arm, fractured skull an fractured ribs, and it was thought that he had been dead for some time.

He was found in the sub-basement by the firm's boiler fireman.

He was last seen on the Saturday 9 January 1943 at about 8.55pm leaving a public house in Liverpool under the influence of drink and saying that he was going home.

He had been seen several times by a woman that lived in Hawthorn Road in Bootle who said that he had been with another Dutch seaman. She said that after he left the public house she never saw him again.

He was a Dutch seaman and a ship's greaser and had been staying at a hostel in Liverpool.

An open verdict was returned.

Baby

Age: 0

Sex: female

Date: 11 Jan 1943

Place: Christleton, Cheshire

The body of a newly-born female child was found on a railway embankment at Christleton.

The body was found by a linesman who lived in Woodlands Drive, Hoole. He said that he had been walking along the Chester to Crewe main line on the Monday 11 January 1943 in the direction of Waverton when, at the Whitchurch Road Bridge at Christleton, he went up the embankment and when he neared the top he found a cardboard box. He said that when he opened one end of the box he found that it contained the body of a child. He noted that he also found some string lying near the box.

A policeman stationed in Christleton said that at about 3.40pm on the Monday afternoon he went to the railway bridge at Christleton and saw the linesman and that at the top of the embankment near the wall of the bridge he found the box that contained the body of the newly born child.

The pathologist that carried out the post-mortem said that the child appeared to have been dead for about five days and said that he thought that the child had lived for at least five minutes.

He concluded that he thought that death was due to lack of attention at birth.

Baby

Age: 0

Sex: female

Date: 9 Jan 1943

Place: North Marine Lake, Southport

The body of a newly born female child was found wrapped up in a brown paper parcel on a wall that sloped down from the promenade at Southport to North Marine Lake.

A doctor that examined the child said that it had breathed for a short while and had been strangled. He noted that the child also had a fractured skull.

He noted that he did not think that the child's birth had taken place under normal conditions.

A verdict of murder against some person or person's unknown was returned.

Frederick James Pollington

Age: 42

Sex: male

Date: 8 Jan 1943

Place: Bury Road, Newmarket, Suffolk

Frederick James Pollington was knocked over by a vehicle.

He had been cycling along the Bury Road at Newmarket towards Bury St Edmunds at about 8.30am on 7 January 1943 when he was run into by an army van which was one of two vehicles that had apparently just passed a third van.

Frederick Pollington was taken to the White Lodge Hospital suffering from serious injuries and died the following day, 8 January 1943. A doctor that treated him said that Frederick Pollington was conscious when he was admitted to the hospital and had told him that he had been run over but didn't know by what. He said that his condition was good until the following day when he suddenly collapsed and died at 12.45pm. He said that his death was due to shock and multiple injuries.

The vans involved didn't stop and it was not known who had been driving them. At his inquest, two representatives of the American Forces were present.

Frederick Pollington had been employed by Messrs. Coulson and Son, builders, in Cambridge and had lived at 17 Hamilton Terrace, Exning Road in Newmarket. His wife said that he had left home on the Thursday morning at about 8am to go to work and had been in his usual good health.

A labourer that lived in Swaffham Road in Burwell said that he had been cycling along Bury Road with Frederick Pollington, coming from Newmarket at about 8.20am on 7 January 1943. He said that when they saw two lorries approaching, they got into single file. He said that he was cycling in front and had his dynamo lighting set on although noted that he could not say whether Frederick Pollington had had his lights on. He said that the two lorries then started to pass other traffic on the road and came too far across the road and that the cloth covering of one of the lorries struck him in the face and that he then heard a crash behind him and then saw Frederick Pollington lying on the left-hand footpath.

He said that the front wheel of his bicycle was broken off.

He said that the two lorries were both military vehicles and apparently American and had bright lights and had been travelling too fast. He added that they didn't stop.

Another person at the inquest said that in their opinion the driver of the lorry involved must have known that they had hit something.

A Post Office engineer who lived at Stanley House Lodge on Bury Road said that he had been walking along the Bury Road towards Newmarket when two lorries passed him very close to their off side, not more than 18 inches from the curb. He said that the first lorry missed a cyclist but that the second lorry hit a cyclist behind. He said that the lorries were travelling not less than 35mph and were of American type.

He said that he could see both of the cyclists quite well when they were 100 yards away and said that the collision was due to the careless way in which the lorries were being driven. He added that he thought that the first driver had seen the cyclist, but not the second.

A flight-sergeant that also witnessed the incident said that he had been walking along the Bury Road and had seen two miniature searchlights. He said that there was then a crash and that the lorries then passed him.

A policeman that arrived at the scene said that Frederick Pollington's bicycle was badly damaged and looked as if a vehicle had passed over its rear wheel. He noted that the road was 28 feet wide.

The police said that enquiries were made, and an appeal was broadcast to trace the drivers of the vehicles, but with no results.

At the conclusion of the inquest the coroner said that it was impossible to identify the vehicle involved and as such, they only had one side of the story. However, he added that there could be no doubt that there had been a considerable degree of negligence on the part of the drivers of the two vehicles

although noted that there was not sufficient
evidence to form an opinion as to whether
the cause of death was accidental or
criminal, and returned an open verdict.

James Patrick OConnor

Age: 38

Sex: male

Date: 7 Jan 1943

Place: Caryl Gardens, Caryl Street, Liverpool

James Patrick OConnor was found dead in a courtyard.

It was thought that he had fallen from a balcony.

He was a dock checker and had lived at 6 Scourfield Street in Liverpool.

He was found dead on the Thursday morning, 7 January 1943 in the courtyard of a block of Corporation tenements in Caryl Gardens, Caryl Street, Liverpool. He was found lying in a pool of blood with a fractured skull and had three broken ribs.

The coroner said that he did not think that the evidence was sufficient to return anything other than an open verdict but said that he could see no reason to believe that it was anything other than an accident.

The police said that James OConnor had been out to several public houses on the Wednesday night and had later joined a group that went off to a house in Caryl Gardens. The house was on the fourth floor of a block of tenement dwellings and was at the top of eight flights of steps.

The police said that they found that James OConnor had left the party at about 10.10pm under the influence of drink and had gone with two other people to the top of the staircase where he was then left alone. The police said that nothing more was known of James OConnor's movements until his body was found the following morning.

The police suggested that he might have, in his drunken state, thought that he had reached the ground floor when he was actually on a balcony 14 feet above it. They also suggested that he might have been looking over the balcony to see how much further down he had to go and had then over-balanced.

The police said that the lowest balcony was about 14 feet from the ground. The police added that there was no evidence of foul play.

Two people that had been at the party said that James OConnor had seemed able to take care of himself when he left and said that when they last saw him descending the stairs he had done so carefully with his hand on the rail and had had called out 'Goodnight'. They added that there had been no trouble at the party.

Baby

Age: 0

Sex: female

Date: 7 Jan 1943

Place: Wilfred Street, Boldon Colliery

The body of a newly born female child was found in a field at the back of Wilfred Street, Boldon Colliery.

The police said that they were called to a field at the back of Wilfred Street in Boldon Colliery at about 1.15pm on the Monday 4 January 1943 where they saw the body of the child wrapped up in a light blue blouse, a towel and some brown paper.

A doctor that examined the child said that he thought that it had been alive from birth for between 8 and 18 hours.

The coroner said, 'This child died due to negligence and exposure caused by a person or persons unknown'.

Stephen Emerton

Age: 68

Sex: male

Date: 3 Jan 1943

Place: North Wharf, Harrow Road, Paddington

Stephen Emerton was found dead in the canal five days after he went missing.

He had lived in Purves Road in Kilburn and was an ARP rescue worker at the North Wharf depot. He was found dead in the canal by North Wharf at Harrow Road in Paddington. His wife said that he had left home on the morning of 28 December 1942 to go on duty for 24 hours, saying that she expected him home at about 8.30am the following morning. She said that when Stephen Emerton didn't return home, she contacted the depot and said that they told her that he had left the depot for home. When he hadn't returned by later that evening his wife reported him missing and his body was later found on 3 January 1943.

It was thought that he had been in the water for at least two days.

His post-mortem revealed that his death was not due to drowning, but from crushing injuries to his chest and it was thought that he might have been crushed between a barge and the canal bank.

The police surgeon that went to examine his body by the canal at 2.30pm on 3 January 1943, said that he had multiple injuries and thought that he had been dead for at least a couple of days.

Stephen Emerton's wife said that Stephen Emerton didn't suffer from loss of memory and said that he was on good terms with everybody.

The man that was in charge of the North Wharf rescue party said that Stephen Emerton had done his job satisfactorily and that he was on good terms with all the other men there. He said that Stephen Emerton had been engaged on special duties which included the distribution of blankets at the depot and that because of his special duties he was exempt from roll call. He said that he came on duty at 8am on 28 December 1942 and that the last time he saw him was at about 7pm.

The man said that the depot premises were alongside the canal but that there was a 10ft high fence along the canal although it did have gaps in it through which access to the canal could be gained. However, he said that Stephen Emerton's duties would not have taken him to the canal bank.

Another rescue worker that was on duty said that during the 24 hours between 28 December and 29 December 1942 that Stephen Emerton had seemed as usual and described him as a happy man.

He said that he would sleep in the store and would go off duty at 8am on 29 December 1942 and that Stephen Emerton came along at about 7.40am and called to him that it was time to get up.

A party leader with the rescue party said that he saw Stephen Emerton leaving the depot yard at 8am on 29 December 1942, saying that he was going out of the lower gate that led into Harrow Road. He noted that

Stephen Emerton had not been wearing his uniform coat when he left.

Another rescue worker that came on duty that morning, 29 December 1942 just before 8am said that he saw Stephen Emerton by the lower gate cross the yard and go into the road. However, he said that he could not say whether Stephen Emerton had had an overcoat with him at the time.

When Stephen Emerton was found in the canal on 3 January 1943, the police dragged the canal by North Wharf where his body was found. They said that he had been wearing trousers, a shirt and a pullover when he was found, but that there was no overcoat, and none was found.

The police said that they made enquiries with barge-owners but said that they could find no reason why Stephen Emerton would have gone to the canal.

When the coroner returned an open verdict at his inquest, he said that Stephen Emerton had died from multiple injuries that had been sustained under circumstances not fully disclosed by the evidence.

Annie Lewis

Age: 39

Sex: female

Date: 2 Jan 1943

Place: The Croft, Warwick Place, Leamington

Annie Lewis died from an abortion on 2 January 1943.

She was the wife of a tar macadam contractor and had lived at The Croft in Warwick Place, Leamington.

She had suffered a miscarriage on 14 December 1942 and later became ill and was later removed on the orders of her doctor to Eversleigh Nursing home on 18 December 1942. When the doctor was later called to see Anne Lewis again at the nursing home on 20 December 1942, he found her in a serious condition, and it was decided that an operation was required and she was removed to Warneford Hospital. However, she later became ill and died on 2 January 1943.

Following her death, two death certificates were issued, with the original one being withdrawn without the consent of the coroner and she was buried on 6 January 1943.

However, her body was later exhumed from Warwick Cemetery on 17 May 1943 after the coroner received an anonymous letter from the Pearl Assurance Company that they had received. In their letter to the coroner the Pearl Assurance Company wrote that a full enquiry should be made into the matter detailed in the letter before they made a payment. It was noted that when Anne Lewis had been examined in March 1941 by a doctor with a view to taking out a policy, that she had told the doctor that she had had six confinements and two miscarriages and that it was in regard to those circumstances and the letter that they felt that an investigation should be carried out. They also contacted the Leamington Police regarding the matter who also made enquiries.

The letter read, 'Dear Sirs, With reference to the claim made by Annie Lewis's husband on the death of his wife, Annie Lewis, late of 28 Warwick Place, Leamington, full enquiries should be made into this matter before payment is made. I state that it is an established fact that Mrs Lewis's death was caused through using an instrument on herself to cause a miscarriage, all done with her husband's knowledge and consent. The later Mrs Lewis's sister and parents have quarrelled over this matter with Annie Lewis's husband, naturally blaming him for instigating and consenting'.

When the coroner was informed, a warrant for Anne Lewis's exhumation was ordered and a post-mortem arranged, with her body being exhumed on 17 May 1943. The coroner noted that the reason for the exhumation was to ascertain the cause of death.

The verdict at the subsequent inquest was that her death was due to uraemia and abortion self-induced.

The coroner noted that the procedure that should have been adopted by the registrar when cases such as Anne Lewis's death were reported, that of death following abortion, whether it was natural or criminal, was that it had to be reported to the coroner. He noted that that was well known to the medical profession and that it was known that the merest breath of suspicion in such cases had to be investigated. He also noted that it was the responsibility of the coroner to determine whether an inquest was held but said that a post-mortem would have undoubtedly been ordered.

At the inquest, the registrar of births and deaths said that when he first received the death certificate from the doctor, it had had the words 'Abortion' on it and said that he had then asked the doctor whether it was a natural one or induced by artificial means. However, he said that the following day, the doctor sent him a note saying that a man that had been treating Anne Lewis as a private patient wished the cause of death to be given as Uraemia and miscarriage, and so the certificate was reworded accordingly and sent to him.

The doctor said that she had initially certified Anne Lewis's death as being due to pelvic cellulitis and septic abortion and said that the registrar himself asked her to substitute the word abortion with miscarriage. The doctor said that at first she declined, but said that after she spoke to the man that had been treating Anne Lewis privately she issued a second certificate stating that the cause of death was uraemia and miscarriage.

However, at the inquest, the registrar said that a state registered nurse was present when he made the call and said that she was prepared to state that all he had asked the doctor was whether the abortion was a natural or forced one.

However, at the inquest, the coroner asked the registrar whether he rang anyone else about the matter and he said that he didn't, although he did admit that he had spoken to the Coroner for Central Warwickshire District whilst talking to him about another matter when he asked when the inquest was to take place, although he said that he could not remember the date that it was due to take place but agreed that it was probably after Anne Lewis had been buried.

After Anne Lewis's body was exhumed from Warwick Cemetery on 17 May 1943 a professor with the West Midlands Forensic Laboratory in Birmingham said that in his opinion, after carrying out a post-mortem, that the first death certificate stating that death was due to pelvic cellulitis and septic abortion was wrong and that in his opinion death was due to uraemia anuria following a blood transfusion and abortion.

When the undertaker was called to give evidence at the inquest, he said that it was first arranged that Anne Lewis should be buried at Milverton Cemetery but that it was eventually arranged that she would be buried at Warwick Cemetery. However, he noted that Anne Lewis's husband had expressed his wish that she should not be buried in Leamington Cemetery.

When Annie Lewis's husband was questioned, he said that Anne Lewis had had six children and that he knew that she didn't want any more but denied that he knew anything about her condition in late 1942. He said that they had been friendly with a woman that lived in Adelaide Road who ran her home as a home for aged invalids and that they would pay visits there. He said that on 15 December 1942 Anne Lewis was far from well and that two days later they called a doctor in. However, it was noted that it was not their doctor, but the doctor of the woman at Adelaide Road. When Anne Lewis's husband was asked why they had not called their own doctor in, he said that they were friends with the woman, and they had met her doctor at her home quite a lot. He said that he didn't know that she was an expectant mother and said that the doctor had told him that a week in a nursing home would put her right.

Anne Lewis's husband added that he had visited Anne Lewis on numerous occasions in hospital, but said that she never mentioned having used an instrument upon herself.

Anne Lewis's sister said that Anne Lewis had told her in December 1942 that it was her intention to take a certain course of action. She said that she told her not to be silly, but said that after the act had been done, that she again commented on its folly and said that Anne Lewis said, 'If I did not do this my husband said he would leave me'. She added that when she saw Anne Lewis in hospital, Anne Lewis said to her, 'I would never have done it had I known what I was going through'.

Anne Lewis's sister said that relations had been good until around Christmas. She said that it was clear that Anne Lewis's husband was having associations with another woman. She said that she also told Anne Lewis's husband that she didn't like the way that Anne Lewis had died. She also noted that Anne Lewis's husband would not tell her or her family where Anne Lewis's funeral was going to be. She said that she said to Anne Lewis's husband, 'If you don't tell us, I shall go to the Chief Constable, because I don't like the way she died'. However, she said that she did in fact end up attending the funeral.

It was heard that the woman that lived in Adelaide Road said that she had had a great deal of experience with elderly people and said that death had occurred in her home on and off and said that more often than not relatives had asked her to carry out the registration of death, which she did in the case of Anne Lewis on behalf of her husband, and with the help of the doctor. She said that when she first went to register Anne Lewis's death the registrar told her that he was not able to register it as he would have to make some enquiries. However, she said that when she saw him the following day, he told her, 'I am pleased to be able to tell you that I can register the death this morning'. The woman said that on both occasions Anne Lewis's husband had been unable to go to the registrars because he was ill in bed with a carbuncle.

When the coroner summed up he said that he thought that there could be no doubt that Anne Lewis procured the abortion by the use of a syringe although he added that the jury might feel that her husband might have known what was going on although added that mere tacit consent did not amount to aiding and abetting.

He also added that it might be felt that there was an underlying motive on the part of some person or persons to prevent the case being reported to the coroner.

The coroner also criticised the registrar of births and deaths, stating that he had exceeded his duty and also suggested that the conduct of the doctor and the man that had privately treated Anne Lewis was not beyond reproach. He also criticised the evidence of the woman from Adelaide Road who Anne Lewis had visited shortly before her abortion, stating that her evidence was most unsatisfactory.

Printed in Great Britain
by Amazon

74161027R00149